Sarah takes on Big Oil

The compelling story of Governor Sarah
Palin's battle with Alaska's 'Big 3' oil
companies, as told by the state's
top oil and gas editors

Kay Cashman & Kristen Nelson

P N A   P U B L I S H I N G
ANCHORAGE, ALASKA

PNA and PNA Publishing are trademarks
of Petroleum Newspapers of Alaska LLC
www.pnapublishing.com

Petroleum Newspapers of Alaska LLC is publisher of Petroleum News,
a weekly oil and gas newspaper, Anchorage
www.petroleumnews.com

Book jacket design by Mariajosé Echeverría-Stewart
Book inside design by Steven Merritt
Cover photo: 2008 © Greg Martin / AlaskaStock.com
Inside photo spread by Judy Patrick Photography
Map by Mapmakers Alaska

Library of Congress
Cataloging-in-Publication Data
Cashman, Kay
Nelson, Kristen
Sarah takes on Big Oil: The compelling story
of Governor Sarah Palin's battle with Alaska's 'Big 3' oil companies,
as told by the state's top oil and gas editors —1st ed. October 2008
www.sarahtakesonbigoil.com

1. Biography   2. United States   3. Economic history and conditions
4. Industries. Land use. Labor   5.Commerce   6. Oil and Gas   7. Finance
8. Public finance   9. Social history and conditions. Social problems. Social reform
10. The family. Marriage. Women   11. Social pathology. Social and public welfare
12. Political institutions and public administration — United States
13. Geology   14. Technology   15. Alaska
CT210-3150 National biography

For information: PNA, Post Office Box 231651, Anchorage AK 99523
ISBN 978-0-9821632-0-7 (hardcover)

Printed in the United States of America by RR Donnelly

First Edition Printing October 2008

Energy

Some find it
Some produce it
Some refine it
All use it

This book is dedicated
to the people of Alaska.

Acknowledgements

A distinguished list indeed...

It takes a community to raise a child, it is said; and we've found it takes a community to create an environment where words can live.

The authors, Kay Cashman and Kristen Nelson, would like to give special acknowledgement to the people who helped make the title Sarah takes on Big Oil possible.

Thanks from Kay and Kristen to:

Mariajose Echeverria-Stewart who did a fabulous job designing the jacket of our book, including its mesmerizing cover.

Steven Merritt who designed and produced the inside pages at a time in his life when the last thing he needed was more work and an impossible deadline.

Judy Patrick who took many of the photos in our book, including the one of she and Sarah Palin baking cookies, and all the beautiful color photos in the center spread.

Brit Lively and **Carrie Wang** at Mapmakers who designed this book's lovely and useful Alaska map.

Daryl Pederson of D&M Photo who took wonderful head shots of us for the book jacket.

Alan Bailey and **Eric Lidji**, Petroleum News staff writers who took over our news beats, as well as did most of the writing for Petroleum News' annual Explorers magazine while we were working on this book.

Rose Ragsdale who assumed the editor's duties at Petroleum News for us, while working on several other projects. (We couldn't have done this without you.)

Contributing writers for Sarah takes on Big Oil, including Petroleum News reprints and inspiration: **Stefan Milkowski, Ray Tyson, Eric Lidji, Alan Bailey, Gary Park and Rose Ragsdale**.

Tom Kearney who designed the graphs inside this book and the ad on Petroleum News Web site.

Dave Nanney, webmaster for www.petroleumnews.com, whose hair-trigger enthusiasm added zest to the creative process.

Don Steinberger, webmaster for www.sarahtakesonbigoil.com, for your patience and excellent design skills.

Marti Reeve for toiling long hours on research, chasing photos and fact-checking. And Garrett for backing her up every inch of the way.

Tim Kikta for his excellent proofreading, despite his cast.

Theresa Collins, Susan Crane, Bonnie Yonker, Heather Yates, Clint Lasley and Shane Lasley for not complaining about the extra work load at Petroleum News.

Lance Lasley who walked Kay's three big dogs every day except Sunday.

Kaitlyn and Alexis who didn't get much Grandma Kay time for almost a month. And **Luke** who didn't get a birthday present.

Trish Harren and John Lasley who encouraged their mother, Kay, at every turn. **Laura Lasley** for her giggles. **Ray Lasley** for not complaining about the absence of care packages.

Mary Mack for making the finances work, and this book possible as our company's first hardcover book.

Shara Sutherlin, for assorted travails as wife of collaborator Steve Sutherlin.

Wadeen Hepworth who kept telling Kay to get back to work.

Pam Rule who supplied Kay with endless amounts of Frequensea and Electric Fire, which kept her healthy and alert despite long, long days and nights.

Dan who helped found and build a healthy Petroleum News, without which this book would not have been possible.

Finally, **Dee Cashman** who boosted Kay's profile at the Los Angeles Times.

And last, but not least,

The Collaborators

While we, the authors, have been engrossed in writing, our collaborators have been hard at work, solidifying our first book, Sarah takes on Big Oil.

A book is more than words on a page, and a good book is more than just words of an author on a page.

A book is a way to share a vision. Our collaborators share the vision for Sarah takes on Big Oil.

To our collaborators, for all they have done to help make a book from the vision, thank you!

A little about them....

Steve Sutherlin—Anchorage

Raised in Anchorage, Alaska, Steve Sutherlin is the former managing editor of Petroleum News. After years of covering industry in Alaska, Sutherlin left the news staff of the paper to open a strategic action agency assisting companies doing business in Alaska and the Pacific Rim. He has clients in the oil and gas, fisheries, tourism, publishing and entertainment sectors. Prior to his career as a journalist Sutherlin worked as a real estate broker, a building contractor, a commercial fisherman, a musician, and an oil field hand.

Candice Ngo—Washington, D.C.

Candice R. Ngo was raised in Delta Junction, Alaska, a town in the rural Interior of the state. She graduated from the University of Colorado at Boulder and spent eight years working on staff within the United States Senate in Washington, DC. She currently resides on the outskirts of Washington in Silver Spring, Maryland.

Amy Spittler—London

Raised in Anchorage, Alaska, Amy Spittler is the former associate publisher of Petroleum News. Spittler left the paper to pursue a master's degree in international marketing and build a client list for her media services company. She is working with Kay Cashman on an 11-book cross-generational fiction series.

Table of Contents

Index

The index for Sarah takes on Big Oil will be available
online on Oct. 31, 2008, at: www.sarahtakesonbigoil.com

Chapter 1

Sarah raises her sword

"Gov. Murkowski is known as someone who keeps his cards close to his chest. This is fine in poker when you gamble your own money, but ... he's gambling public assets and ... claiming to have won the game while refusing to put all the cards on the table to prove it."

—gubernatorial candidate Sarah Palin, April 25, 2006

By Kay Cashman

T he title of this book, "Sarah takes on Big Oil," is somewhat of a misnomer. As governor of Alaska, Sarah Palin's battle has primarily been with the state's three largest oil producers, BP, ConocoPhillips and ExxonMobil, and their supporters in the state's business community.

Most of the other oil and gas companies have liked Palin's requirements for state support of a North Slope natural gas pipeline, although none of them were happy with the production tax hike she initiated in late 2007.

Alaska Gov. Frank Murkowski, 2002-2006

But the tax fight wasn't a fight Sarah Palin started, even though, as governor, she had to finish it.

The battle began on Feb. 21, 2006, when her predecessor, Republican Gov. Frank Murkowski, introduced legislation that would overhaul the state's oil and gas production tax.

The Production Profits Tax bill, which needed the approval of the Alaska State Legislature, was the product of the Murkowski administration's negotiations with BP, ConocoPhillips and ExxonMobil for a gas pipeline fiscal contract.

Alaska Gov. Sarah Palin, 2006-?

The governor's goal was to get Alaska's "Big 3" oil companies to build a 1,715-mile gas pipeline that would run south from the North

Slope to Alberta, Canada, where an existing pipeline system would take Alaska's gas to Lower 48 markets. (The three producers already controlled—by virtue of majority ownership—the 800-mile trans-Alaska oil pipeline that carried all of the North Slope's oil to market via the Port of Valdez in Southcentral Alaska.)

The fiscal contract negotiated by the Murkowski administration wouldn't compel the three North Slope producers to build a gas line, but it would require them to proceed with "diligence," which was defined as "prudent under the circumstances," to determine whether the project was commercial by their internal standards. In other words, there were no firm requirements to do anything.

When asked whether he thought the producers would move forward and build a gas line, Murkowski essentially said he trusted them to do just that with the incentives he had offered them in the contract. (By February 2006, the three North Slope producers had invested at least $125 million in studies related to a North Slope gas pipeline project.)

But Sarah Palin, who was challenging Murkowski for governor in the 2006 election, disagreed with his tactics.

"We've got to play hardball with these guys," she said in an editorial in her hometown newspaper, the Mat-Su Valley Frontiersman. "They are looking out for their bottom line, and we need a governor who will do the same thing for Alaska."

No tax hikes for 45 years

The fiscal contract had been negotiated under the terms of the state's Stranded Gas Development Act and, as such, had to be ratified—a straight yes or no vote—by the Legislature.

The governor also wanted the Legislature to pass some amendments to the stranded gas act that would make some of the contract's provisions legal. For example, he wasn't allowed to include oil taxes in his gas line negotiations with the Big 3.

Together the proposed Production Profits Tax, the gas line fiscal contract and the stranded gas act amendments would have provided the three North Slope producers with fiscal certainty, a major component of which was fixed rates on their taxes and royalties.

The proposed freeze on taxes and royalties was for 35 years on gas and 45 years on oil. For gas the freeze would begin when the pipeline started up and for oil when the Legislature ratified the fiscal contract. Because the pipeline would take about 10 years to build, it was essentially 45 years for both.

But the tax freeze on oil did not depend on the gas line getting built.

As part of the state's deal with the three North Slope producers, Murkowski agreed to reimburse them with tax and royalty credits for any additional taxes or royalties levied against them—by state and local governments—during the 45 years. (Eventually this provision would apply to all oil companies shipping natural gas in the line because constitutionally they couldn't be excluded.)

Rep. Eric Croft

Rep. Harry
Crawford

Reimbursement was the only way current elected officials could assure the Big 3 of certainty on tax and royalty rates because under Alaska's constitution they couldn't prevent future Legislatures from increasing taxes and royalties, but they could contractually bind the executive branch of government to issuing reimbursements in the form of credits that could be used against their royalty and tax payments.

Rep. David
Guttenberg

Fiscal certainty of this magnitude was necessary, BP, ConocoPhillips and ExxonMobil said, because the gas line was a massive, $20 billion-plus project that was financially risky. They were looking to the State of Alaska to reduce much of that risk, and they were particularly concerned that once the line was under construction the state or local governments along the pipeline route might increase taxes, which the state had done with production taxes in 1976, the year before the trans-Alaska oil pipeline had begun operations.

Where is the North Slope?

Northern Alaska consists of five distinct geologic regions: The North Slope, which is the Arctic coastal plain that stretches across the entire top of the state, including the coast of the Arctic National Wildlife Refuge (ANWR) to the east and the coast of the National Petroleum Reserve-Alaska (NPR-A) in the west. The North Slope stretches south to the second region, the foothills of the Brooks Range, also referred to as the Arctic or North Slope foothills. The Brooks Range is the third region, and the Beaufort and Chukchi seas are the fourth and fifth regions. The Chukchi Sea lies between northern Alaska and Russia, north of the Bering Strait. Offshore the community of Barrow the Chukchi Sea transitions east into the Beaufort Sea, which lies off the northern Alaska and Canada coastlines. The Beaufort and Chukchi seas lie on the margin of the Arctic Ocean. (See Alaska map in the center of this book.)

Gas reserves tax in the works

There was already a new tax under consideration—a gas reserves tax that would be on the ballot in November 2006, spearheaded by Alaska Representatives Eric Croft, D-Anchorage, Harry Crawford, D-Anchorage, and David Guttenberg, D-Fairbanks. In order to generate public debate before the initiative went to voters in November, the three legislators had also introduced a gas reserves tax bill in the Alaska Legislature.

In the 1960s and 1970s the North Slope of Alaska "was a place like no other from which oil had yet been recovered. The technology did not exist for production in such an environment. Normal steel pilings would crumble like soda straws when driving into permafrost," wrote Pulitzer Prize-winning author Daniel Yergin. Photo taken in 1968 at the Prudhoe Bay State No. 1 well.

If approved by Alaska voters in November, the gas reserves tax would have increased the Big 3's tax hit by $1 billion per year until gas started flowing through a pipeline from the North Slope to outside markets.

The proposed gas reserves tax would disappear when the pipeline was built and would have refunded most of the payments after a tax-payer's gas was flowing through a pipeline. But the opportunity to get a refund would have expired in 2030, so the message was clear: "Get busy and build a gas line."

Murkowski and the industry said a gas reserves tax would, in fact, do the opposite of what was intended, sparking lawsuits and raising red flags with the top executives of the Big 3 companies about fiscal stability in the State of Alaska.

Murkowski's chief of staff, Jim Clark, told the Associated Press that if the initiative was approved by voters in November, Murkowski's fiscal gas line contract would shield BP, ConocoPhillips and ExxonMobil from paying the tax because of the agreement's reimbursement provision. Nonetheless, he said if a gas reserves tax was approved by voters it had the potential of killing the gas line project.

The 800-mile trans-Alaska oil pipeline starts at Prudhoe Bay on the North Slope and ends at the Port of Valdez, where oil is loaded onto tankers for shipment to the Lower 48 states.

Republican gubernatorial candidate Palin, who had filed in October 2005 to run against Murkowski in the August 2006 primary, was also opposed to the proposed gas reserves tax because she saw it as poor public policy, "taxing income before it is even earned."

But she also spoke out against Murkowski's willingness to freeze all oil and gas taxes and royalties for 45 years.

Need Big 3's gas to start gas line

According to ExxonMobil, Alaska's 4.5 billion-cubic-foot-a-day gas line would require 57.5 trillion cubic feet of natural gas to keep it full for 35 years.

Why did Murkowski, who had two major pipeline companies very interested in building a North Slope gas line without billions of dollars in fiscal concessions, want the Big 3 North Slope oil producers to build the line?

In a word: Gas.

Despite the fact that government estimates put northern Alaska's undiscovered, technically recoverable natural gas at more than 200 trillion cubic feet, the only major supply of gas that could definitely be ready to produce in the 10 years it would take to build a pipeline was in the Prudhoe Bay oil field, which was controlled by BP, ConocoPhillips and ExxonMobil.

Prudhoe, the largest oil field in North America, held a whopping 24.5 tcf of natural gas. Combined with the 9 tcf in the discovered-but-undeveloped eastern North Slope's Point Thomson field that was controlled by ExxonMobil (36 percent), BP (32 percent), Chevron (25 percent) and ConocoPhillips (5 percent), the three major North Slope producers had enough gas to keep the pipeline full for at least half its life.

Gas monopoly concerns

But some state leaders did not want the North Slope's gas production to be dominated by the Big 3, as it had been with oil.

Until recent years BP, ConocoPhillips and ExxonMobil had kept tariffs (tolls) on the trans-Alaska oil pipeline high enough to keep out other oil companies, except in the form of minority interests in their North Slope fields. As a result, they controlled all the oilfield facilities and related pipelines in northern Alaska. Their production companies had to pay the same per-barrel tariff as other companies, but they could essentially get their profit back on the other end because it was their pipeline subsidiaries that owned the oil line and the service company that operated it, Alyeska Pipeline Service Co.

Even Conoco, before it merged with Phillips (which had bought ARCO Alaska's assets) had left the state after discovering and developing an oil field, complaining that the oil tariff charged by the owners of the trans-Alaska oil pipeline was unnecessarily high and made it impossible for other companies to make a reasonable profit on northern Alaska fields, especially compared to elsewhere in North America and the world.

Conoco developed the Milne Point oil field but pulled out of the state in January 1994 after selling the field to BP.

In 1994 Conoco and Tesoro began—and Tesoro, Anadarko Petroleum, Flint Hills and the State of Alaska continued—successful legal action against the owners of the trans-Alaska oil pipeline. Their efforts eventually led to a reduction in intrastate oil (oil that was used in Alaska) tariffs in 2004. A 2008 ruling by the Federal Energy Regulatory Commission, or FERC, led to a reduction in interstate tariffs retroactive to 2005.

As of September 2008, the tariff battle was still being waged and would likely see higher court action. But the owners of the trans-Alaska oil pipeline appeared to be losing and would likely have to refund hundreds of millions of dollars in overcharges and pay additional state taxes because the lower the tariff rate, the more the state collects in taxes.

Palin prefers independent gas line

As governor, and while she was campaigning for governor, Palin expressed concern about the Big 3 owning the gas line because of their actions as owners of the oil pipeline.

The 2008 FERC ruling, she said in June 2008, supported the idea that an independent pipeline company, and not the Big 3, would be the preferred builder of the proposed gas pipeline.

"This decision shows how having a pipeline constructed and operated by the producers can result in inflated tariff rates that cause the State of Alaska significant revenue losses and discourage others who do not own a share of the pipeline from developing the state's resources," Palin said as governor.

Others maintained that the predecessors of BP, ConocoPhillips and ExxonMobil were the only companies willing to take a chance on Alaska's North Slope in the early, very risky, pre-Prudhoe-discovery years when others were pulling out of northern Alaska, and so deserved their preferred position.

The chicken and the egg

The problem facing the state with the gas line was the proverbial chicken and egg dilemma. Before companies would put $50 million into a remote gas exploration well they wanted to be sure a pipeline to major markets was going to be built. But in order to get financing, a pipeline company would need proven gas reserves that could be brought online in sufficient quantities to fill a pipeline.

Companies that had exploration acreage in the gas-prone Brooks Range Foothills and elsewhere in northern Alaska were reluctant to move forward with gas exploration until they were certain there would be a pipeline to take the gas they found to market. Otherwise, their gas would be stranded. (Previous gas discoveries in northern Alaska were either accidental finds in the search for oil or were discovered when looking for small deposits of gas for local use.)

Even the Big 3 were not exploring for natural gas in 2006 or, for that matter, in 2007, 2008 or 2009 (plans for northern Alaska's exploration drilling season, which is in the winter when the ground is frozen to protect the tundra, had already been established early October 2008 when this book went to press).

Tom Irwin

Exploration and development of a gas field was expected to take seven to 10 years; a pipeline 10 years, including engineering and permitting.

So the only game in town was Prudhoe Bay. And, to a lesser extent, Point Thomson because of the size of its reserves and the number of wells already drilled in the field.

But in 2006, Point Thomson was on the verge of litigation between its leaseholders and the State of Alaska, which would decide to take it back because no wells had been drilled in the eastern North Slope field since the 1980s, and work commitments (drilling, etc.) had not been met by the field operator, ExxonMobil. What would happen with Point Thomson had not been decided when this book went to press, although the Palin administration had won the first round in court.

Thus, expectations were that Prudhoe Bay would produce the first natural gas for a pipeline; hence the need to involve BP, ConocoPhillips and ExxonMobil at some point in any gas pipeline plans.

More importantly, the three producers had made it clear to the Murkowski administration that they would not sell their gas to a third party. They wanted to build and hold controlling interest in the gas line because it was in their best interests to do so. (The heads of BP, ConocoPhillips and ExxonMobil have a fiduciary responsibility to do what is best for their shareholders.)

Some experts, including former state Division of Oil and Gas director Mark Myers, said the Big 3 were bluffing; that their shareholders would not allow them to sit on a multibillion dollar gas resource if a pipeline was available to carry it to market.

Producers in strong bargaining position

Control of Prudhoe Bay's gas put the Big 3 in a strong bargaining position with the Murkowski administration.

The unfortunate thing was that Alaska's CEO put himself and his "shareholders," the citizens of Alaska, in the exact opposite position by starting his negotiations with the producers by saying "I want to have this done by September."

Alaska Department of Natural Resources Commissioner Tom Irwin, who was fired by Murkowski and who returned as DNR commissioner under Palin, reflected on the situation in a September 2008 interview with Petroleum News: "When I go into negotiations with someone on something, little or big, and the other side tells me I want to have this done by September, you know what I think on the other side of the table? There is no way you're going to get what you want by September. Because I've immediately got a very strong hand because you've got time dependency and I don't. You're immediately behind in the negotiations. It lets the other side know you've got a timeline, you're desperate. And why would I want to hurry?"

From 12.5 to 20 percent

Murkowski said his proposed Petroleum Profits Tax, or PPT, would increase the state's income by $2.6 billion in the years 2007 through 2012.

Why would Alaska's Big 3 oil companies ask for a tax hike as part of the gas line deal?

They wouldn't—and didn't.

The three North Slope producers initially asked the governor for a 12.5 percent tax rate with a 25 percent tax credit for investment, but after one of the administration's outside oil and gas consultants publicly recommended a 25 percent tax rate and the governor prom-

From left, Tony Hayward, BP Group's managing director and chief executive officer of exploration and production; Alaska Gov. Frank Murkowski; Morris Foster, president of ExxonMobil Production Co.; Jim Mulva, chairman of the board and CEO of ConocoPhillips; and Murkowski Chief of Staff Jim Clark at the Feb. 20, 2006, meeting in Alaska.

ised the Legislature that his PPT bill would carry a 25 percent rate, top executives from the companies' corporate headquarters flew to Alaska to meet with Murkowski and Clark on Feb. 20, 2006.

The governor postponed presenting his bill to the Legislature until he could meet with the oil executives, who included London-based Tony Hayward, BP Group's managing director and chief executive officer of exploration and production who would eventually take John Browne's place; Houston-based Jim Mulva, chairman and chief executive officer of ConocoPhillips; and Houston-based Morris Foster, president of ExxonMobil Production Co.

Murkowski said he had made up his mind to drop the PPT rate to 20 percent before he met with the big guns from the three companies, an assertion that was met with skepticism by several legisla-tors, but the following day he announced the Big 3 producers had agreed to a 20 percent tax rate and the principal provisions of a gas pipeline fiscal contract.

The Big 3 producers had to know going in that a tax increase of more than their 12.5 percent rate was likely if a rewrite of the state's production tax was put in front of the Legislature. Contrary to pub-lic opinion, industry's record of pushing through new legislation in Alaska was dismal.

What they had been be very good at, however, was stopping or mitigating legislation that was harmful to their bottom line. That was before Palin took office in December 2006, and before federal indictments began coming down against some of their strongest supporters in May 2007.

Some not convinced

Several legislators—even some industry-friendly Republicans—thought the production tax rate should be at least 25 percent. They also complained that Murkowski's bill had too many tax breaks, espe-cially since the price of natural gas and oil had more than doubled since 2000.

On Feb. 23, 2006, the Alaska Budget Report, published by Juneau, Alaska-based ABR Co., reported it was "hard to find a tax break that drafters of the legislation left out." The article noted a last minute change by Murkowski that would delay the effective date by six months, saving Alaska producers about $390 million.

The publication, which closely followed the Legislature, also protested the "delightfully arbitrary $73 million" that each oil compa-ny got to add to its expenses any year it made a profit.

"How many bites of the apple do we give people?" asked Tom Wagoner, the Republican senator who chaired the Senate Resources committee, a sentiment shared by another Republican committee member, Fred Dyson, who was worried Alaska was going to "get the short end of the stick" because of "all the credits, look-back and invest-ment incentives" in the new production tax.

Alaska's shrinking ELF

Still, most legislators wanted a change in the production tax, because the field-based gross tax that was in place at the time—the Economic Limit Factor system, commonly known as ELF—was bringing in less and less revenue each year, with tax rates falling as pro-duction declined.

In 1993 the average North Slope production tax was 13.5 percent.

In 2004 it had fallen to 7.5 percent.

By 2015, the Alaska Department of Revenue predicted it would fall to about 1.5 percent.

Already the second largest field in the

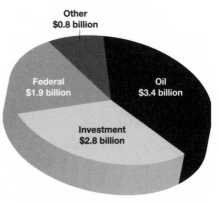

FY 2005 Total Revenue: $8.9 billion

Other
$0.8 billion

Federal
$1.9 billion

Oil
$3.4 billion

Investment
$2.8 billion

Courtesy Alaska Department of Revenue - Tax Division
Spring 2006 Revenue Sources Book

United States, the North Slope's Kuparuk River unit, was paying no production tax under ELF, even though it was producing about 46 million barrels of oil per year—a gross value of about $2.6 billion in early 2006 when PPT went to the Legislature.

And some newly discovered smaller oil accumulations such as the 19,000-barrel-a-day Tarn field were able to take advantage of Kuparuk's zero tax rate because its oil was processed at the Kuparuk facilities before being shipped down the 800-mile trans-Alaska oil pipeline.

The decline in production tax revenue was of huge concern to

Alaskans because oil revenues—production tax, corporate income tax, property tax and royalties—funded most of the state's General Fund unrestricted revenues. Most legislative and public debate centered on this category of revenue which, simply put, was divided up annually by the Legislature and the governor to run state government.

When the other major contributor to Alaska's coffers, the federal government, gave money to states it restricted how that money could be used. Highway and airport construction funds, Medicaid and education funding could not be used for other purposes. In addition to restricting how the money was spent, the federal government often required states to put up matching funds to qualify for federal funding.

Alaska's Oil Fiscal System by Source FY 2005

Total — $3.631 billion

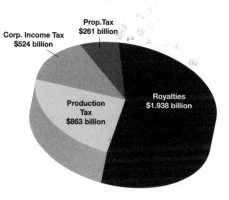

Corp. Income Tax $524 billion

Prop. Tax $261 billion

Production Tax $863 billion

Royalties $1.938 billion

Alaska Department of Revenue Sources Book, Fall 2005
Property taxes include municipalities
Royalties include Permanent Fund

In the state's fiscal year 2005, oil revenues made up 89 percent of the state's unrestricted revenue—$2.9 billion out of a total $3.2 billion. Oil also directly contributed another $546 million to the state's $3.2 billion restricted revenue, and indirectly part of the $2.6 billion in the form of earnings from the Alaska Permanent Fund.

Not to belittle the investment prowess of the Permanent Fund's managers, but the fund wouldn't exist without the annual royalties collected by the State of Alaska from oil and gas leaseholders.

It was established in 1976, a year before completion of the trans-

Alaska oil pipeline from the newly developed Prudhoe Bay oil field on the North Slope to the Port of Valdez. A voter-approved constitutional amendment required the state to put 25 percent of its oil, gas and mining bonuses, royalties and related income each year into the special fund for placement in income-producing investments.

As of September 2008, about 46 percent of the Permanent Fund's principal had come from the petroleum industry. As of closing Sept. 18, 2008, the market value of the fund stood at $34.2 billion.

The Permanent Fund is an investment fund that has taken its seed money from petroleum dollars and built them into a renewable financial resource. In addition to the fund's current balance of $34.2 billion, which is $20 billion of investment earnings on $13 billion of oil money, it has also paid out more than $16 billion in dividends to individual Alaskans. (Read more about the Permanent Fund in the last chapter of this book.)

Each year the Alaska Department of Revenue publishes a "Revenue Sources Book" to give the governor, Legislature and public a summary of past state revenue collections and a forecast of future revenue. In February 2006, when the governor introduced his new production tax proposal, the most recent Revenue Sources Book said oil revenues would make up just 85 percent of Alaska's unrestricted revenue through FY2008, a four percent drop from FY2005, and fall to 75 percent in FY 2009 through FY 2011.

So, the majority of Alaskans were open to a new tax system or, at least, to revising ELF.

In addition to Alaskans being concerned about less and less revenue under ELF, the increase in oil prices from $20 a barrel in 2001 to $50-plus in 2006 produced a whole new desire to get more money when oil prices were higher. (Oil companies were paying the same tax rate at $8 per-barrel oil as they did when oil was $100 a barrel with ELF.)

The Big 3 said the reason they agreed to a 20 percent tax rate versus the 12.5 percent they initially asked for was because they wanted the gas line contract and related stranded gas act amendments ratified by the Legislature.

Heeding Lord Browne

The challenge was finding the right balance so that the final tax bill would be a win-win for the industry and the state.

But many legislators questioned whether Murkowski's version of a new production tax provided that balance. Most lawmakers were up for re-election in November 2006, so they were under additional pressure to get PPT passed because it was tied into the governor's proposed gas line fiscal contract with the three producers. No one wanted to be accused of holding up the gas pipeline.

After PPT was introduced to the Legislature on Feb. 21 the top BP, ConocoPhillips and ExxonMobil executives in Alaska warned legislators that the tentative pipeline deal they had struck with the Murkowski administration could fall apart if legislators revamped the governor's PPT legislation in any way, especially by raising the tax rate.

But Murkowski's tax bill was betting Alaska's future revenues on high oil prices. According to modeling done by Alaska Department of Natural Resources consultant Econ One, it would take something in the neighborhood of a sustained $50-per-barrel price to get what the state had made in 2005 from production taxes.

JUDY PATRICK

Lord John Browne, BP

If the price of oil fell under $21 per barrel, the state would get no production revenues, Econ One said.

The Alaska Department of Revenue was forecasting lower oil prices for the rest of 2006 through 2008, and an average of just $25.50 per barrel for 2009 and beyond.

Revenue wasn't alone. The 2006 U.S. Energy Information Administration energy outlook report forecasted $47 per barrel through 2025.

Worse, later in the legislative tax debate, BP's chief executive in London, Lord John Browne, would tell the Guardian Unlimited that he thought it was "very likely that, in the medium term, prices will stand at about $40 on average."

Browne's prediction sounded reasonable because when Murkowski introduced PPT toward the end of February 2006, the daily price of West Texas Intermediate crude oil had been dropping. After opening the month at $68 per barrel, price levels had moved steadily downward as supply reports showed increasing inventory levels. The average price for February was $55.82 per barrel. (In 2001 and 2002, the average price of West Texas Intermediate crude oil was about $26 per barrel; $31 in 2003; $41 in 2004; and $56 in 2005.)

Rep. Les Gara

Adding fuel to the fire, Rep. Les Gara, D-Anchorage, a long-time advocate of production tax reform, introduced an alternative tax bill that carried a 30 percent tax rate. He reminded his fellow legislators that in 2004 Browne had said at $20 per barrel BP made so much money it gave the excess cash flow back to shareholders.

In an April 15, 2004, address to shareholders, Browne had indeed said, "In periods of high oil prices such as the one we find ourselves in today, the group generates significant 'excess free cash flow' after capital expenditure and dividends. Rather than using this cash to reduce debt … we are committing to return … 100 percent of this excess free cash flow to our investors, for as long as oil prices remain above $20 a barrel, all other things being appropriate."

Browne reaffirmed that policy in 2005.

"We're … not going to give money back to oil companies when they're making huge profits," Gara said in early 2006. He said his party's bill made sure that the production wouldn't reduce the oil company's tax liability above $20 a barrel.

Reprint from the Sept. 28, 2008 Petroleum News. The world of oil and natural gas prices is never a sure bet. Here's the latest threat to the economic viability of a gas pipeline from Alaska's North Slope to markets in the lower-48 states.

Shale sinks gas prices

Tech advances, greater investment in unconventional resource fuel U.S. glut

By Ray Tyson
For Petroleum News

It's no mystery that increasing supplies of natural gas in the U.S Lower 48 have contributed to serious erosion in gas prices. Perhaps less obvious is that major technological advancements in tools that better extract gas from the numerous shale deposits underlying the continent, which are easy to find but can be difficult to produce from, have contributed to the price deterioration.

Since hitting a high of $13 per thousand cubic feet in the early part of July, natural gas prices have plummeted more than 40 percent to their current level of around $7 per mcf.

A GLANCE FORWARD

In fact, the market is so awash in natural gas that Chesapeake Energy, among the largest gas producers in the United States and a major shale player, announced Sept. 22, 2008 that it planned to reduce its drilling budget during the second half of 2008 through year-end 2010 by $3.2 billion, or 17 percent, in response to the price decline and concerns of "an emerging U.S. natural gas surplus …"

Just how long this price downturn will last, and whether it threatens any long-term conventional gas projects, such as Alaska's proposed

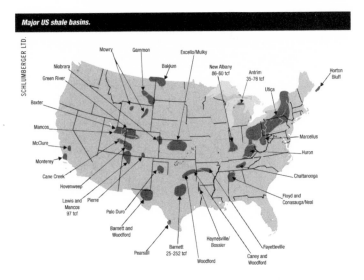

Major US shale basins.

SCHLUMBERGER LTD.

gas pipeline system, is anybody's guess. It largely hangs on future demand, which some hope will lead to a mass conversion to natural gas vehicles and gas-fired industrial plants to reduce America's dependence on oil imports.

U.S. gas reserves up 50 percent?

A recent study by Navigant Consulting for the American Clean Skies Foundation concluded the United States has up to 50 percent more natural gas reserves—or 2,247 trillion cubic feet— than some earlier projections because of higher-than-expected yields from 22 shale formations in 20 states.

U.S. domestic gas production, a good indicator of where prices are headed, at least in the short term, was up 8.8 percent in the first half of this year compared with the same period a year earlier. That rate of increase was last seen in 1959, during the great drilling boom that followed World War II.

Read the rest of the story online at:
http://www.petroleumnews.com/pnads/849058035.shtml

Chapter 2

Sarah and the Magnificent 7

"Somehow, the governor and industry think (a 45-year freeze on oil and gas taxes) ... is perfectly reasonable. Yet no one would suggest with a straight face that industry freeze gas and oil prices for decades."

—Mat-Su Valley Frontiersman, Sarah Palin's hometown newspaper, spring, 2006 gubernatorial campaign

By Kay Cashman

By far, the biggest issue overshadowing the tax debate in 2006 was the secrecy surrounding the gas line fiscal contract that the Murkowski administration had negotiated with the Big 3 producers, BP, ConocoPhillips and ExxonMobil.

The governor wanted the Alaska Legislature to pass his new Production Profits Tax, or PPT, before the end of the legislative session at midnight on May 9, without seeing the fiscal contract, even though Gov. Frank Murkowski said PPT was an integral part of the deal he had struck with the three North Slope producers. (PPT would tax oil company profits at a rate of 20 percent while granting a 20 percent tax credit on reinvestment.)

Sarah Palin

It irked many legislators, as well as gubernatorial candidate Sarah Palin, that the governor would not release the contract until the Legislature passed his tax bill.

The Stranded Gas Development Act, under which the fiscal contract had been negotiated, provided for a private dialogue between the governor's office and companies interested in building a pipeline, but the secrecy was wearing thin with Alaskans and their lawmakers, especially since the governor had said the contract gave the producers a 45-year guarantee on all their state and local tax and royalty rates.

The debate began on Feb. 21, 2006, when Murkowski introduced PPT to the Alaska State Legislature, and at the same time announced he had reached an agreement on the major provisions of a gas pipeline fiscal contract with the state's Big 3 oil companies.

"To have an agreement on both is historic," he said at an Anchorage press conference he had called for the occasion.

Details of the contract were still being worked out, the governor told reporters, and the fiscal contract itself would not be released until his PPT bill had passed the Legislature.

He told reporters that a bi-partisan group of legislative leaders—including House Speaker John Harris and Senate President Ben Stevens—had met with the heads of the three companies on Feb. 20.

The oil executives included Tony Hayward, BP Group's managing director and chief executive officer of exploration and production; Jim Mulva, chairman and chief executive officer of

Frank Murkowski

ConocoPhillips; and Morris Foster, president of ExxonMobil Production Co.

Murkowski called the meeting between lawmakers and the company heads "a very, very healthy dialogue where the legislative leadership got an opportunity to ask questions and get, I think, reassuring answers."

At the meeting legislators said they had made it clear that the Legislature would have the final say on oil taxes.

"You can negotiate with the administration all you want, but in the end you have to negotiate with us because we determine state law," recounted Harris, a Republican from Valdez, after the meeting.

According to an Anchorage Daily News report, Stevens, R-Anchorage, and son of U.S. Sen. Ted Stevens, R-Alaska, said the company executives "were optimistic about future investment in Alaska, and we said obviously we're interested in the future development of Alaska's natural resources. It just has to be a fair and equitable arrangement."

Rep. Ethan Berkowitz, the House minority leader, said he was encouraged by what he heard at the Feb. 20 meeting.

"The Senate president and the speaker told them we're not negotiating, and oil was going to be considered separately from gas," Berkowitz was reported as saying in the Anchorage Daily News. "They were very strong on that front."

In a press release from the governor's office after the Feb. 21, 2006, press conference, Steve Marshall, president of BP Exploration (Alaska) Inc. called the deal with the Murkowski administration "a significant milestone" and said he was "pleased to have completed the gas portion of the fiscal contract" and was "working to finalize durable oil contract terms" that "incorporated the new oil tax structure."

"We see the merit in a profits-based oil tax system, provided it appropriately balances risk and reward to enable additional investment," Marshall said.

Jim Bowles, president of ConocoPhillips Alaska, was also pleased that "all parties" had "reached an agreement in principle with the State of Alaska on the base fiscal contract terms for an Alaska gas pipeline project," noting that company officials believed a "well-constructed net profits tax could benefit Alaska and provide the fiscal certainty that will support future investment."

Richard Owen, vice president of ExxonMobil Alaska Production Inc., said the "oil contract terms consistent with the governor's proposed tax bill would provide the predictability and durability necessary to advance the gas project to the next phase," confirming that the company had "reached agreement with the governor on the major provisions of the gas fiscal contract."

Owen said he looked forward to "working with the administration to finalize the materials and initiate the public comment period."

Murkowski, Clark enthusiastic

"This is basically what I came back from the United States Senate to accomplish in Alaska, to get the economy moving, and a significant portion of that was the dream of marketing our gas," Murkowski said at the press conference, referring to his previous 22 years in the U.S. Senate.

Clark, who had led Murkowski's gas team in the negotiations with the Big 3 companies, told reporters that it was "one of the happiest moments" of his life when the major provisions of the gas pipeline fiscal contract were completed.

But the gist of the contract would not be released until after PPT had passed the legislature, he said, outlining a three-step process.

Jim Clark

First, he said, PPT had to be passed by the Legislature before it adjourned the regular session.

Second, probably in a special session after the regular session, the administration would introduce a "package of amendments" to the stranded gas act, Clark said. The amendments were things not allowed under the stranded gas act, such as including the tax freeze on oil in the contract with the gas producers.

The Legislature, he said, would receive the proposed fiscal contract with the three North Slope producers at the same time it received the amendments, and would be able to look at them side by side in a special session. (Some amendments were introduced or discussed earlier.)

The PPT legislation and the stranded gas act amendments would need to be passed, Clark said, before the Legislature could have an up or down ratification vote on the contract. (In other words, the Legislature would not be allowed to change anything in the agreement; just vote yes or no on it.)

Murkowski told reporters that he was looking for a balance between revenues to the state and incentives for the companies. He said his choice of a 20 percent tax rate and a 20 percent credit rate in the bill was tilting the balance "a bit ... in favor of creating new incentives" because, aside from the 1002 area of ANWR, "we're unlikely to find major discoveries of the Prudhoe Bay size."

Selling Alaska's oil for "peanuts"

State Rep. Eric Croft, D-Anchorage, attended the governor's Feb. 21 news conference.

According to the Anchorage Daily News report, after the conference ended Croft "hotly debated Clark about Murkowski's oil tax plan. The two were face-to-reddening-face, like a baseball manager with an umpire."

Croft, who was running for governor, "took Clark to task over the need for confidential negotiations and the level of the proposed oil tax," the newspaper reported.

"I think it's a sad day," Croft told the Associated Press. "One hundred thirty-nine years ago Russia sold Alaska for peanuts, and we just sold Alaska's oil for peanuts. I think we're going to get a gut check on this Legislature and finally find out who owns this state."

Sarah says wait for gas line contract

In an opinion piece in her hometown paper, the Mat-Su Valley Frontiersman, Palin asked legislators to hold off voting on the production profits tax until they had seen the gas pipeline fiscal contract.

"Gov. Murkowski is known as someone who keeps his cards close to his chest," she wrote in another opinion piece. "This is fine in poker when you gamble with your own money, but it's very dangerous when it's other folks' assets put at risk. Murkowski claims he was victorious in crafting a deal with three big oil companies to build a natural gas pipeline through Canada, but now says he won't disclose what's in the deal. Until we see otherwise, it appears he's gambling public assets and ... claiming to have won the game while refusing to put all the cards on the table to prove it."

That same hometown paper, which would later endorse Palin

after she beat Murkowski in the Republican primary, also criticized Murkowski for what it aptly described as "a decades-long freeze" on oil and gas production tax and royalty rates: "Somehow, the governor and industry think this is perfectly reasonable. Yet no one would suggest with a straight face that industry freeze gas and oil prices for decades," the Frontiersman said.

Tax needs to be revised, with or without gas line

But some legislators, such as Rep. Ralph Samuels, R-Anchorage, the co-chairman of the House Resources Committee, thought the tax legislation stood on its own even if a pipeline agreement was not made public.

According to an Anchorage Daily News report, Samuels became frustrated while running committee meetings, trying to keep the discussion on the proposed PPT legislation off the gas pipeline contract.

Fairbanks Republican Rep. Jay Ramras, the other Resources co-chair, told the newspaper that they were doing all they could to keep the two issues separate.

"It may be a consideration for the producers in the context in which they came to the table, but as far as the House Resources Committee is concerned, we've built a long, tall brick wall between the gas pipeline legislation, which we may or may not get, and (the oil tax legislation), which will stand on its own," Ramras was quoted as saying.

Chuck Logsdon, Alaska's former chief petroleum economist

Logsdon on Alaska's geology

Chuck Logsdon was one of the people who testified in favor of Murkowski's PPT legislation.

The state's former chief petroleum economist told legislators that the 20 percent rate was fair and appropriate for Alaska, even if oil prices went back up to January 2006 levels. At the end of January, West Texas Intermediate crude oil had been about $68 per barrel, whereas when the PPT debate began in the Legislature on Feb. 22, the price had dropped about $12 per barrel.

Logsdon reminded legislators that one of the governor's goals was to encourage exploration because oil production from the maturing fields in Alaska's main petroleum region, the North Slope, was in decline.

The state's total oil production had dropped from more than 2 million barrels of oil a day in the late 1980s to less than a million barrels a day in 2006, and all indications were that it would drop even lower without substantial investment. (By mid-2008, production had dropped to 700,000 barrels a day. Alaska's other oil-producing region, the Cook Inlet basin in the Southcentral part of the state, was also in decline, producing only about 13,300 barrels of oil a day.)

Logsdon told legislators they needed to remember what the onshore geology in Alaska likely held—i.e. no more giant, 15 billion-barrel oil fields like Prudhoe Bay, except possibly in the 1002 area of the Arctic National Wildlife Refuge, which was off limits to oil and gas exploration and development.

If Alaska's geology had large, low-cost fields close to market, the state could "probably take a huge government take and still get plenty of investors coming in," Logsdon told legislators.

But that was not the situation with Alaska. The state had a regressive fiscal regime, or taxing structure, and did not offer enough incentives to offset its high-cost environment.

Alaska, he maintained, could change its system with PPT to both increase its government take and encourage investment, something many other oil and gas provinces had done around the world.

Logsdon said the state had a portfolio of North Slope projects that weren't economic to develop and produce even at higher oil prices.

High oil and gas prices were not enough to draw exploration investment to the state because prices were high everywhere, he told them.

"If we can't improve our relative competitiveness" with other states and countries that have geological prospects similar to Alaska's, "we're really not that much better off" with high commodity prices, he said.

Traditionally, large fields were found and developed first and then companies went back to develop smaller, challenged fields.

"So one of the ways of trying to keep yourself closer to (production) growth than maturity is to provide the kinds of incentives to go out and try to put these smaller pieces together," Logsdon said.

Palin says it's easy: Heed the Constitution

A year later, in 2007, Alaska Gov. Sarah Palin and former Gov. Walter Hickel at a press conference in the governor's mansion in Juneau, the state's capitol.

On March 19, 2006, Sarah Palin penned another opinion piece in her hometown newspaper, the Mat-Su Valley Frontiersman, offering advice to Alaska's lawmakers.

This time she wrote about the Alaska Constitution, the "good book" she adheres to in public office, and reportedly keeps close at hand.

Industry negotiators, she wrote, "are some of the sharpest professionals on earth, with decades of experience dedicated to their company's bottom line. Our negotiators are citizen legislators or political appointees who sometimes are dependent on industry for their next job."

It might look like Alaska is "outgunned at the table, but thankfully we can compete because we've got supremely powerful ammunition. It's called the Alaska Constitution, and it provides our strength as we deal with corporations whose ultimate goal is to

Sarah says, "I'd hire them"

While campaigning for the 2006 gubernatorial election Sarah Palin wrote about the loss of seven Department of Natural Resources officials in a guest editorial in the Mat-Su Valley Frontiersman, her hometown newspaper.

In October 2005, "a superb team of top DNR officials left Gov. Murkowski's administration after they inquired, confidentially, into the legality of aspects of ongoing gas line negotiations. That these valuable Alaskans were lost is shameful," Palin wrote.

"They should be ushered back to state service so we might again benefit from their expertise and integrity. I'd hire them."

The "experienced team walked away from the gas line negotiations and the Murkowski administration, believing the 'deal' was not in Alaska's best interest," Palin wrote.

Alaskans "recognize that oil executives seeking maximum revenue for their shareholders are simply doing their job. More power to them. Industry should not be criticized for fulfilling fiduciary duties, providing Alaskans jobs and revenue in the process.

"But it takes an equally intelligent administration to ensure that Alaskans are neither taken advantage of nor denied our fair share. Alaska's 'CEO' must possess the same savvy and steely nerves to use constitutional leverage to bring Alaska and the oil companies together into a mutually beneficial agreement to tap and market our resources," Palin wrote.

make themselves maximum profit" and leave little behind, Palin wrote.

"I respect industry's contributions to our economy as it pumps our oil, gets it to market and makes a mind-boggling profit off our resources. I personally appreciate the blue-collar job opportunities industry provides. I am, in fact, married to a (North) Slope worker, so I'm not out to bash industry, nor do I expect officials to use a hammer in negotiations. But I do expect us to stop acting weak and confused and just do the right thing for Alaskans, via our Constitution," she continued.

Favorite Sarah quote

"Let me help you out if you're looking for skeletons in my closet. I got a D in a macro-econ course 24 years ago in college (and) hollered at the wrong kid this morning for not taking out the garbage."

—Sarah Palin, The Associated Press, August 2006,
during Alaska gubernatorial campaign

Quoting the Constitution, she said, "Negotiate for the maximum benefit of all Alaskans. Period. That must be the objective. It really is that straightforward."

Officials, Palin said, could make it easier on themselves by committing to not let "politics, cronyism or campaign cash get in the way."

"Remember one's oath of office where one is sworn to defend the unequivocal terms mandating development and conservation of natural resources for the maximum benefit of all Alaskans. Not outside interests, but Alaska's interests," she wrote, asking state officials to "negotiate from our position of strength."

"As former governor Walter Hickel wrote, 'Legislators should simply hold up a copy of Article VIII and say, I swore to uphold this document, I'll keep my promise.' Legislators need only defend the public's interest and they'll inherently do what's right.

"It's amazing to consider the perspective our founding fathers had when crafting the Constitution. ... What they knew to protect may not have been fathomed in their wildest dreams whilst writing the document, but I believe their concerns are manifesting today with these negotiations," Palin wrote.

Alaskans, she said, deserved to be listened to because their resources were on the table.

Her message to lawmakers: "Use restraint, don't rush decisions that have long-lasting impacts. Don't tie oil taxes to a gas line contract that isn't even available for scrutiny."

To the governor she wrote: "Trust the public with all the information. Don't let companies hide behind confidentiality, handing them control of our revenue by undefined terms and undeveloped credits. Don't give retroactive credits to stimulate investment decisions made years before, as 'retroactive incentive' is an oxymoron. Make financial models public.

"Simply, let us trust you to uphold your oath to defend our Constitution," Palin advised.

What if oil prices dropped?

Mark Myers, the state's former oil and gas director, was opposed to PPT, and not just because it would become part of a secret gas pipeline fiscal contract.

Myers said April 15, 2006, in a speech to a pro-development group in Anchorage, that Murkowski's proposed overhaul of the state's production tax could spark giant legal battles with some of the world's most powerful energy companies and posed a downside risk to the state if oil prices reverted back to their traditional price range.

Murkowski's plan to tax oil profits marked a huge potential change to the current system, which based the tax on the value of the oil at the wellhead.

The state didn't have the large and expert bureaucracy needed to calculate the true profits and costs. Nor did it have the pay structure to attract and retain the experts it needed, Myers said.

Myers was among seven top officials in the Alaska Department of Natural Resources who left the Murkowski administration in October 2005. They said the governor was giving up too many financial concessions to the oil companies in negotiating a natural gas pipeline fiscal contract, and disagreed with the proposed restructuring of production taxes.

Converting the state's entire production tax to a profits-based, or net, system could provoke ongoing legal wrangling over what defines profit and production costs, Myers said, particularly since the "governor's bill contained significant ambiguities in what are allowable deductions and profits."

As the state's director of oil and gas, Myers had managed the state's net profit share oil and gas leases.

For "previous directors and me they were an auditing and accounting nightmare. The net profit share component time and time again significantly underperformed the state's expectations. Given that long history of underperformance, I find it odd that the Department of Revenue, which has never managed a net profit system, is so optimistic," he said. "Do you want a system that's going to lead to war between the companies and the state?"

Myers also said PPT was a huge risk for the state if the price of oil went down.

The modeling by Econ One, he said, "clearly" showed that "under the administration's proposal at prices less than $30 dollars a barrel the state will receive less than projected under the current system looking forward. ... If oil prices were to fall to the $20-$30 range the state could have little to no severance (production) tax, one-half to one-third the current royalty dollars and much lower corporate income tax revenue at the same time it may be attempting to invest billions of dollars in the gas line (under Murkowski's contract the state would have been a 20 percent owner and would have had to pay its share of the cost of building the line).

AL GRILLO

Dan Dickinson

"How will we pay for government if this happens? Will a general income tax be proposed or will the Permanent Fund be raided?" he asked.

Gubernatorial candidate Sarah Palin agreed with Myers, and went on record as preferring a tax on the gross sale of oil and gas, versus a tax on the net, or profits.

A few skirmishes

Dan Dickinson, an accountant and former state tax director, disagreed with Myers and Palin. He said PPT would allow the state to

Placards bracket Alaska gubernatorial candidate Sarah Palin as she addresses a rally in Anchorage May 5, 2006, that protested the secrecy of the gas line contract with Alaska's Big 3 producers and Murkowski's proposed change in the state's production tax.

accurately gauge oil company profits and collect taxes.

Murkowski's tax plan would prevent oil companies from disguising profits as production costs, said Dickinson, who was working for the Murkowski administration on the oil tax issue. It included a list of items companies could not count as production costs, ranging from depreciation to donations to fines.

"There are going to be some skirmishes around the fringes," he said. "I believe that 95 percent of the costs will be without controversy."

He acknowledged that the state did not have the team of auditors it would need to collect the taxes.

"We would have to build a team," Dickinson said.

As the PPT debate waged in the Legislature there was a proposal, which was ultimately defeated, that inserted a floor in PPT that would have protected the state at low oil prices.

Administration and legislative consultants had said all along that when you replaced a regressive system with a progressive system the proportion of the government's take increased at high prices but could drop to zero at low oil prices: If the companies had no profit, there would be no profit to tax. The Murkowski administration testified that one good year would make up for several bad years.

Palin joins protest rally in Anchorage

The secrecy issue just wouldn't go away. More and more people wanted to see the gas line contract.

On May 5, 2006, Palin joined 200 activists and politicians outside the state headquarters building in Anchorage to protest the secrecy of the gas line contract with the Big 3 and Murkowski's proposed change in the state's production tax.

The event was organized by All Alaska Alliance director Lori Backes, who put together a similar rally in Fairbanks the next day.

Palin and former Gov. Walter Hickel were among the speakers, asking legislators to hold off voting on a new production tax until Murkowski made the gas line deal public.

Former DNR Commissioner Tom Irwin, out of state visiting his mother, called into the rally on speaker phone.

"It's truly looking like a secret process. Maybe even an orchestrated and manipulated process," he was quoted as saying in the Anchorage Daily News.

Backes was part of a Fairbanks-based group promoting an all-Alaska natural gas pipeline—i.e. a route that would follow that of the trans-Alaska oil pipeline to Valdez where the gas would be converted to liquefied natural gas, or LNG, and shipped by tanker to markets outside the state.

Two months earlier she had penned a guest editorial that appeared in several Alaska newspapers (see copy at the end of this chapter), criticizing Murkowski's plan for building a pipeline, and pointing out that Alaska oilfield service company VECO and its executives were the state's largest source of oil industry campaign money and appeared to have "undue influence" over the political process in Juneau.

Backes also listed 11 legislators who received the most VECO money, which led to some of them joking about being members of a

"Corrupt Bastards Club," and making up caps with a CBC logo.

Another lawmaker, Senate President Ben Stevens, was also mentioned by Backes as receiving consulting fees from VECO. (In 2006, he had received more than $240,000 from VECO since 2000.)

According to the Anchorage Daily News article, earlier in the week, Alaska Support Industry Alliance general manager Paul Laird sent an e-mail to Alliance members, dubbing the rally a publicity stunt and encouraging members to send lawmakers a different message regarding the gas line: No delays.

"Tell them we've waited long enough," Laird wrote.

Judge forces Murkowski to reveal contract

Between Feb. 22 and May 9, 2006, the last day of session, committees in both the House and Senate spent countless hours taking testimony about PPT from the Murkowski administration, their own and the administration's consultants, the state's oil and gas producers and explorers, and the public.

Eventually both the House and Senate passed the bill, but not the same version.

Sen. Tom Wagoner, R-Kenai, like Sen. Gary Wilken, R-Fairbanks, objected to the oil industry's advertising campaign around the PPT legislation, and said he wished there was time to take the bill to a conference committee and work out differences between the House and Senate. He said he thought the tax change was needed, but couldn't vote for the bill until there had been more work done on it.

Hollis French

After months of debate, the effort to revise Alaska's production tax system floundered in the last days of the regular legislative session, a victim to politics, the complexity of issues involved, the mandatory end of the legislative session, and especially a victim to the governor's refusal to release the gas line fiscal contract, which many legislators wanted to see before they approved a new production tax.

Mark Myers

Marty Rutherford

Tom Irwin

Dick LeFebvre

Not pictured: **Nancy Welch**

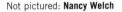

But the governor was not allowed to keep the gas line contract secret.

In May 2006, in French v. Murkowski, Sen. Hollis French, D-Anchorage, filed a lawsuit

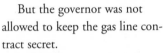

Bill Jeffress

Bob Loeffler

seeking immediate release of the gas line contract.

Juneau Superior Court Judge Larry Weeks issued an order on May 5, 2006, for the contract to be released.

The governor did not make it public until May 10, one day after the legislative session closed.

The 'Magnificent 7' make their mark

Lending even more fuel to the fiery debate over the Production Profits Tax and the gas pipeline fiscal contract it would be imbedded in, were seven former members of Gov. Frank Murkowski's administration. One of them, DNR Commissioner Irwin, had been fired by the governor in late 2005.

The other six members of the "Magnificent 7" were top level DNR officials who quit in protest of Irwin's dismissal and the governor's handling of the gas line negotiations with Alaska's three major oil producers, BP, ConocoPhillips and ExxonMobil.

The public brouhaha started when Irwin, concerned over the direction of the state's gas pipeline negotiations with BP,

ConocoPhillips and ExxonMobil, wrote to Attorney General David Márquez Oct. 20, 2005, asking for legal advice on a number of issues. (The departments of Revenue, DNR and Law were all involved in negotiating the fiscal contract.)

To Irwin's surprise, the governor released his internal memo Oct. 21 and put him on administrative leave Oct. 22. Irwin was fired Oct. 27.

The six senior DNR officials immediately resigned in protest, including deputy commissioners Marty Rutherford and Dick LeFebvre, oil and gas division director Mark Myers, division of mining director Bob Loeffler, office of project management and permitting director Bill Jeffress, and Nancy Welch, one of three special assistants in the commissioner's office.

They were dubbed 'The Magnificent 7' by division of oil and gas employees who hummed the tune from the movie as the departing officials walked through the division's offices saying farewell to employees.

Murkowski deal not good for state

In October 2005 letters to the governor, the six DNR officials said they were resigning because of the dismissal of Irwin and the administration's position in the gas pipeline negotiations with the Big 3 North Slope producers, BP, ConocoPhillips and ExxonMobil.

The resignations were effective Nov. 15, 2005, "or sooner at your discretion," as Rutherford put it in her letter.

Jeffress, LeFebvre, Loeffler and Welch said they regretted resigning but had no alternative following Irwin's dismissal.

"Unfortunately, I am unable to support the direction of the administration and believe it is necessary to take this action," all of them wrote.

Letters from Rutherford and Myers were more detailed.

"I regret that I must take this action but I feel I have no alternative following the dismissal of Tom Irwin ... and the position the administration has taken in negotiations regarding a North Slope gas pipeline," Rutherford wrote. She was two years away from state retirement at the time, having worked for the state for 23 years under six governors. Her most recent 10 years of state service was as deputy commissioner under both Republican and Democratic governors,

"Supporting the administration's position would require me to accept terms clearly not in the interest of the state," Rutherford wrote, adding she was proud of the work the department had done in pursuit of a natural gas pipeline and that she believed "the action I have taken today is necessary to avoid that effort going to waste."

Myers also expressed his displeasure with the governor's dismissal of Irwin.

"I adamantly disagree with the administration's current position on gas line negotiations. … Staying in this position would require me to compromise my values as to what is right, both legally and ethically, and what is in the interests of the state," he wrote in his letter of resignation.

Myers, a former employee of ARCO Alaska, had been with the state for more than 11 years, five as director. (In 2006 Myers was appointed the head of the U.S. Geological Survey, or USGS, which is part of the Department of the Interior in Washington, D.C.)

"As you know," Myers told the governor in his letter of resignation, "I adamantly disagree with the administration's current position on gas line negotiations. While I appreciate the offer to remain in my position while avoiding all work associated with gas line negotiations, I do not believe that scenario is feasible. The current negotiations have implications that permeate every aspect of the state's oil and gas interests now and into the future. I cannot continue as director and watch silently as the state's interests are undermined by creating barriers for the new oil and gas participants that are so vital to the economic future of the state."

After announcing his departure from DNR, Myers told Petroleum News, "One point we wanted to bring forward is we're baffled that the governor is only moving forward one contract. With the TransCanada and port authority options available to him, why isn't he moving all three forward so that the Legislature and the public can consider them?"

A spokesman for TransCanada told Petroleum News that the company had reached a conceptual agreement with the state in the spring of 2005.

But until the fiscal contract was released by the governor, the Magnificent 7 could not comment on any part of it, except what the governor and his people had already publicly discussed.

A confidentiality agreement would effectively silence them until the contract was released.

Gas line economic without subsidies

What was wrong with the gas line fiscal contract?

The list was long, and many of the items on it would become part of Palin's list of things-not-to-do when she became governor.

One complaint the three lead DNR officials were able to reference was the amount of incentives in the contract. Some estimates said the deal would cost the state $10 billion over a 45-year period; others said if oil prices remained high, in the $60 per-barrel range, the amount would be closer to $60 billion.

Rutherford put the number at $13.25 billion, without including several aspects of the contract that she couldn't reference or were difficult to measure.

"My whole background's in economic development," said Irwin, who did the economics on a North Slope gas project himself, and "I am strongly and absolutely convinced this is an economic project" without incentives.

The DNR team working on the project reached the same conclusion, he said, as did Econ One, a firm hired by the Legislature in 2005 to look at the project.

Read the contract, Irwin said in a presentation with Rutherford in June 2006 after the gas line contract was released by a court order, and then "approach it from a business perspective."

Studying gas prices would have met due diligence standard

Irwin said his conclusion was that the companies, not the state, had gotten a good deal.

"The state gets no deal," he said. First, the producers could get out of the contract in 60 days—the state had no way out short of proving that the producers had not met a diligence standard to move ahead with the project. Studying gas prices could have met that test, he said, and kept the State of Alaska tied to a 45-year exclusive deal with the Big 3 producers.

"It's a good deal for them. We have no deal," Irwin said.

The contract also removed the state's sovereign authority, he said: "Would you, with your company, remove your authority in a contract?"

Irwin said he believed that giving up the state's option to take royalty in kind or royalty in value was "an absolute mistake" and created significant cost and risk issues for the state, putting the state "in a position of weakness in getting capacity in the lines" and in competition with the best marketers in the world to sell the gas.

We're now told, he said, that another company would sell the gas for us. But under the current system, the state didn't pay for the service and it got the highest price of any seller.

And if the state was going into this as a business, Irwin said, Alaskans needed to see the real costs, "not the political feel-good" cost.

He said it appeared a higher gas price was used in discussing revenues—without costs deducted—and a lower price when discussing supports needed for the project. In business dealings both parties use a range of prices, he said.

The facts needed to be put on the table so that everyone could answer the question: "Would you sign this if it was your business?"

Rewrite of state's position

In the same June 2006 presentation, Rutherford said there were more than incentives in the contract.

"This contract is a total rewrite of our entire oil and gas relationship with the producers," turns the existing oil and gas leasing program on its head and "largely surrenders the power of all three arms of government, our sovereign powers, to the producers."

The Legislature would lose its power to tax the producers for up to 45 years; the "executive branch loses its right to manage and regulate the producers' oil and gas leases and the ability to ensure those leases are adequately and appropriately developed" for up to 45 years; and the "judicial branch loses the ability to oversee the contract enforcement for up to 45 years."

Forty-five years is a long time Rutherford said, "and that alone, in my mind, is an unacceptable risk. Nobody thought that when ... the ELF (economic limit factor on the state's production severance tax) was passed 15 years ago, that we were implementing a flawed taxation structure on our oil and gas leases. And yet, within 15 years, that's what we discovered: it is a flawed structure."

The period of time the contract was locked in was "far too great a risk for us to accept," she said.

The cost of contract subsidies

Rutherford said the fiscal contract would have set up a system that was "a total destruction of our normal, competitive environment" for oil and gas leasing, allowing the producers to lock up some 500 leases on the North Slope for the term of the contract, "for 45 years, if they meet that weak diligence standard ... which does not require building a pipeline or doesn't require significant investment into a pipeline."

The state also would lose its ability "to ensure that leases are developed in a timely manner should they be economic," she said. The contract created a two-class system that would have discouraged investment by companies that wouldn't have had those advantages.

Rutherford said Econ One had determined that with no state

incentives and the producers owning 100 percent of the project under the fiscal system that was in place at the time, that if natural gas sold for "$4 the producers have a 17.2 percent rate of return;" at $5, it would have been 20.4 percent.

Rutherford compared that to a 15 percent rate of return oil companies generally used as a benchmark.

Then there was a $13.25 billion cost to the state to sign the contract, "independent of its own investment in the pipeline," Rutherford said, which at a $4 gas price was a direct subsidy to the producers, independent of the state's ownership position, worth "over half the value of the state gas." At $3 gas, the state's position was negative. "So we are writing a check in order to produce our gas."

Compare that to the status quo, she said: If the price of natural gas goes below the transportation cost—but the state is taking its gas in value, rather than in kind—"we don't get a check, we pay zero, but we don't actually go negative."

The risk at low prices was one that would alarm any company, she said.

Palin beats Murkowski, PPT passes

After two 30-day, back-to-back special sessions, on Aug. 10, 2006, the Alaska Legislature passed a 22.5 percent net production tax with a 20 percent tax credit. Initially referred to as the Petroleum Profits Tax, the legislature kept the initials but called the new tax the Petroleum Production Tax.

Murkowski signed PPT into law three days before Palin beat him in the Aug. 22, 2006, Republican primary election, and 11 days before FBI agents raided the offices of six Alaska legislators with search warrants looking for financial ties between the lawmakers and oilfield service company VECO.

A copy of one of the search warrants, obtained by The Associated Press, linked the federal investigation to the new production tax law and the natural gas pipeline contract Murkowski had negotiated with

Sarah Palin: Republican maverick for governor

In the 2006 race for   vernor of Alaska, Sarah Palin cast herself as a Republican maverick, continuing her battle with party leaders that began in 2004 when she was appointed chair of the Alaska Oil and Gas Conservation Commission.

In her position on the three-person commission she reported ethics violations by fellow commissioner Randy Ruedrich, who was the chairman of the Alaska Republican Party.

Ruedrich owned up to leaking a confidential memo to an oil company lobbyist and conducting party business from AOGCC's office.

He was fined $12,000, the largest fine ever levied in an ethics case.

In 2005, Palin teamed up with Democratic lawmaker Eric Croft, also a gubernatorial candidate, to file an ethics complaint against Alaska Attorney General Gregg Renkes, who had served as an aide to Murkowski while he was a U.S. senator from Alaska. Renkes eventually resigned.

But Ruedrich had not resigned as party chairman, and Palin would have to work with him to get party support.

See the rest of the story in chapter 3.

Sarah Palin and Judy Patrick baking cookies. How does Palin manage it all? The kids, family, responsibilities of elected office? "She doesn't do anything else. It's all kids and work. ... Her idea of a big night out is a barbecue in her backyard," said Patrick, a close friend of Palin's.

the three North Slope producers.

According to the warrant, included in the items to be seized were "all documents concerning, reflecting or relating to proposed legislation in the state of Alaska involving either the creation of a natural gas pipeline or the petroleum production tax." VECO and its executives had aggressively promoted BP, ConocoPhillips and ExxonMobil's position on both.

The incumbent legislators whose offices were raided who had been identified as members of the Corrupt Bastards Club were Senate President Ben Stevens, former House Speaker Pete Kott, Chairman of the House Special Committee on Oil & Gas Vic Kohring, and Senate Rules Committee Chairman John Cowdery. All four were Republicans. (As of Oct. 1, 2008, Kott, Kohring and Cowdery had been indicted, as had Ben Stevens' father, U.S. Sen. Ted Stevens, whose trial started at the end of September 2008. Kott and Kohring are currently serving jail sentences.)

Many attributed the corruption investigation, which the FBI would only describe as "ongoing" at the time, to Backes' March guest editorial, but Petroleum News sources said it had been in the works for almost a year.

Ray Metcalfe, a former legislator and the founder of the independent Republican Moderate Party, had been trying to get the authorities interested in what he described as the "corrupt" relationship between VECO and the Republican-led Alaska Legislature, especially Stevens.

"I put all the stuff in front of federal prosecutors a year and a half ago," Metcalfe told the Anchorage Daily News the day of the raids, which were executed in Anchorage, Juneau, Wasilla, Eagle River and Girdwood. "I laid hundreds of pages of detailed information alleging bribery, and I distributed it to federal authorities, I distributed it to the U.S. Attorney's office, I distributed it to the (state attorney general's) Office of Special Prosecutions, and we held a demonstration in front of the attorney general's office that hardly anyone showed up for."

Metcalfe attempted to open a recall campaign against Stevens, but his request was rejected by Lt. Gov. Loren Leman on legal grounds. Stevens, who had said he was going to run for re-election in November 2006, changed his mind in June and said he was going to retire from the Legislature.

IN PRINT

Reprint first published in the Anchorage Daily News as a "COMPASS: Points of view from the community" piece on March 3, 2006, and republished in September of that year.

Follow money to governor's gas deal

By Lori Backes

After watching the legislative hearings on Gov. Frank Murkowski's bill that would completely restructure our oil and gas taxing system, I am baffled that certain legislators are arguing that we must pass this as is, right now, without amendment, or risk scuttling the governor's gas line deal.

OPINION

As the Legislature conducts an unprecedentedly aggressive schedule of hearings on this legislation, Rep. Norman Rokeberg called the contention that the oil industry exercises undue influence over Alaska politics a "myth."

Is it?

According to APOC reports, the most prolific and consistent "investor" in Alaska politics is the oil industry. The employees of VECO Corp. stand out as the largest contributing block. Between 1998 and 2004, reports show that VECO employees and their family members contributed no less than $914,929 to Alaska political campaigns. The following totals represent the amount of donations received from only the top seven VECO executives:

- Senate Rules Committee Chair John Cowdery: $24,550.
- Rep. Pete Kott, former speaker of the House: $21,300.
- House Rules Committee Chair Norman Rokeberg: $18,000.
- House Oil and Gas Committee Chair Vic Kohring: $14,708.
- Gov. (Frank) Murkowski: $6,500 (not including donations to his U.S. Senate races).

- House Finance Committee Co-Chair Kevin Meyer: $12,300.
- House Finance Committee Co-Chair Mike Chenault: $12,000.
- House Judiciary Committee Chair Lesil McGuire: $12,000.
- Senate Labor and Commerce Committee Chair Con Bunde: $11,500.
- Senate Finance Committee Co-Chair Lyda Green: $9,000.
- Rep. Mike Hawker: $8,050.
- House Labor and Commerce Chair Tom Anderson: $8,000.

One should note that these totals do not include Senate President Ben Stevens' "consulting" contract with VECO; Rep. Meyer's salary and benefits from Conoco Phillips; or the salary, retirement and stock options to the Rep. Hawker household from Conoco Phillips. Also, Rep. Hawker was apprised of confidential gas line contract negotiation information while under contract to ASCG Inc., a subsidiary of NANA Development Corp., which has contracts for oil field services with VECO and BP.

This is not intended to pick on any particular legislator. Many Alaskans make their living off the oil industry, and many individuals and organizations donate to political campaigns. But it does show how much VECO and the producers are willing to invest in our state government.

Have these financial linkages and political investments afforded "undue influence" over Alaska's political players and process? Perhaps not, but certain actions might suggest otherwise....

Read the rest of the story online at: http://dwb.adn.com/news/government/veco/story/8149575p-8042343c.html

---

"With Frank Murkowski and Ben Stevens in charge, it's like the Night of the Living Dead. We're being guided by two people whose political careers are over."

—Sen. Hollis French, D-Anchorage, Petroleum News, Aug. 27, 2006

Chapter 3

Sarah Palin: "Take a stand"

In 2006, when she was running to unseat then-Gov. Murkowski in the Republican primary, Sarah Palin got a call from Ben Stevens, then president of the Republican-run Alaska Senate and son of U.S. Sen. Ted Stevens, R-Alaska. "He told me, 'You're not just running against Murkowski. You're running against me, my dad, the whole state Republican party.'"

—Gov. Sarah Palin told the Wall Street Journal in September 2008

By Kay Cashman

With the cloud of corruption surrounding the new production tax system and the failed gas line contract, public sentiment toward the oil industry in Alaska took a huge hit in 2006.

In some ways the year was worse than 1989, when the Exxon Valdez tanker grounded on Bligh Reef in Prince William Sound and spilled nearly 11 million gallons of oil across the sound, into the Gulf of Alaska to Kodiak Island and beyond.

That disaster did many things, including kill some 250,000 seabirds, 2,800 sea otters and 300 harbor seals. It also damaged the reputation of Alaska's oil and gas industry outside the state, ending any chance of opening the 1002 area of the Arctic National Wildlife Refuge to oil and gas exploration.

But it didn't put a reformer with the backbone and conviction of Sarah Palin in the governor's mansion. In fact, 10 years after the Exxon Valdez spill a Dittman Research poll showed 95 percent of Alaskans believed that oil and gas development had been good, or very good, for the state.

It took the fiscal contract negotiated by the Murkowski administration with BP, ConocoPhillips and ExxonMobil, and the new petroleum production tax, or PPT, for Alaskans to choose a maverick Republican with no statewide office experience over an incumbent Republican governor who had served the state for 22 years in the U.S. Senate.

Companies asked for too much

"The companies went too far, they asked for too much in the gas line deal with Murkowski; and it turned around and bit 'em in the ass," one of Petroleum News' solid industry sources said after Palin was elected.

"She's going to bring every one of them back. Every one she can," he said, the day after the election, referring to the six senior Department of Natural Resources officials who resigned in 2005 when then-Gov. Frank Murkowski fired DNR Commissioner Tom Irwin. "And they're not going to let the companies get away with it again," he said, referring to the seven DNR officials and their opinion of Murkowski's proposed fiscal contract with the three North Slope producers.

But what if the North Slope's natural gas wasn't needed in the Lower 48 states in 10 years? What if increasing supplies of natural gas from the huge shale deposits underlying the continent become easier and more economic to produce due to technological advancements? What if plentiful gas supplies cause gas prices to fall and make the cost of shipping gas from Alaska too expensive?

A lot could change in 10 years, which was the time it would take to build a pipeline from the North Slope to the existing pipeline system in Alberta, Canada. Didn't the uncertainty of gas demand and prices warrant major financial concessions by the State of Alaska?

"They're going to need some major tax breaks, sure, and fiscal certainty, too, but not 45 years' worth, and not a situation where state agencies and courts have no jurisdiction and where the producers control the arbitration process ... three owners against the state's one vote. If they would have stopped asking for more just because they could get it—just because Clark (Murkowski's chief of staff, Jim Clark) would give it to them—say, two years ago (2004),

Definition of upstream, midstream, downstream

The oil and gas industry is usually divided into three major parts: upstream, midstream and downstream.

Upstream refers to those operations that involve exploration, development and production of oil and gas, including the drilling of wells.

Midstream is a term used to describe the storage and transportation of oil and gas, including pipelines and tankers.

Downstream often refers to both midstream and downstream operations, because it is loosely defined as the commercial oil and gas operations beyond the production phase. But, technically, it's only the refining and sale of oil and gas products, such as gasoline and gas stations.

the state would have said yes to their deal. Back then there wasn't anyone in the Legislature or anyone in the Murkowski administration, except maybe Mark Myers (one of the six DNR officials who resigned), who would have argued against 60 percent of what was in that contract, maybe 70 percent. But they're learning ... and soon the companies won't be able to hoodwink any of them except, maybe, through campaign contributions or consulting fees. That tends to create blinders.

"Now they've got Sarah Palin. And they're in for the surprise of their lives," he said. "She's as tough as any of their negotiators, even Massey (Martin Massey, ExxonMobil). ... She's going to get the best deal she can for Alaska. It's a sea change in how things ... are done up here."

The oil company executive just quoted asked not to be identified when he first made his comments, and again for this book. He worked for one of the Big 3 oil companies, which controlled—by virtue of majority ownership—all of the oil production facilities and pipelines in northern Alaska in 2006, and still did in 2008, with one small, and recent, exception.

But this author asked similar questions of non-facility and non-pipeline-owner oil companies doing business in northern Alaska in 2006; some holding gas-prone acreage in northern Alaska and hop-

Murkowski's list of missteps

Nearing the end of his first term as governor of Alaska, Frank Murkowski didn't file for re-election until four days before the June 1, 2006, deadline.

His approval ratings were the second lowest in the nation in mid-2006, and according to Alaska pollster David Dittman, the governor's approval rating had slid from 35 percent in late 2005 to 21 percent by July 2006.

The former four-term U.S. senator from Alaska had made a lot of missteps since he'd come home to be governor. He ran on a no-tax platform but soon after he took office he proposed a sales tax. He slashed the longevity bonus to senior citizens, almost as sacred as the Alaska Permanent Fund dividend to the citizens of the state.

Then he appointed his daughter Lisa Murkowski to fill his term in the U.S. Senate, passing over Fairbanks businessman John Binkley and the former two-term mayor of Wasilla, Sarah Palin, both of whom filed to run against him in the 2006 Republican primary for governor.

And all that on top of an unpopular gas line fiscal contract and new production tax.

ing to get their gas into a pipeline. Most of their answers, albeit not as colorful, were as strong about Palin and the three North Slope producers. They did not like the Murkowski contract, but they did like Palin's AGIA and the license that had been issued under AGIA to TransCanada, or TC Alaska.

Prudhoe oil spill the last straw

The industry took other hits in 2006, too, all of them setting the stage for the election of Sarah Palin on a reform ticket on Nov. 4.

In March of that year, there was a 200,000 gallon spill at the nation's largest oil field, Prudhoe Bay, which BP operated.

The company managed 1,273 miles of pipelines across Prudhoe Bay, but the 16 miles of key "oil transit lines," major trunk lines that funneled crude oil into the trans-Alaska pipeline and were the site of the 2006 leaks, were an afterthought. BP's corrosion control unit was fractured into "town" and "field" units, and until the leaks occurred no one took "ownership" of the transit lines, which carried pure oil and no corrosive water, and thus were viewed as invulnerable to holes caused by corrosion.

A "spill" on the North Slope could technically be as small as a quarter cup, and most spills were saltwater, not oil. Anything larger than a gallon, by law, had to be reported by the field operators—i.e. BP and ConocoPhillips—and cleaned up.

Typically, the North Slope operators were "conservative in their reporting procedures and tend to report oil spills of any size," Bob Mattson of the Alaska Department of Environmental Conservation told Petroleum News Oct. 3, 2008.

You couldn't even park a vehicle in the Prudhoe Bay unit and several other North Slope oil fields without placing a pan under the engine to catch stray drops of fluids—a policy that had been put in place by the companies, not the government.

But the spill at Prudhoe Bay in March 2006 was the biggest ever in northern Alaska's oil fields.

Worse, a second leak, discovered in August 2006, led to a partial shutdown of the field, driving up world oil prices, and was blamed, in part, on cost-saving measures BP had established during the years of low oil prices in the 1990s, when Prudhoe production was also in steep decline.

Fed up with politics as usual

It was a perfect time for a reform candidate, who came in a smart, attractive, fearless package: Sarah Palin.

Not only was the stage set for a reformer, but Palin seemed to do everything right, winning against major odds by first unseating a sitting governor who was strongly supported by her own party, and then by beating a former two-term governor, Tony Knowles, with as much charisma as she had and a lot more experience.

Palin was fed up with the good old boy network. She'd come up against something similar in the Matanuska Susitna Borough while mayor of Wasilla, and although that network was not party affiliated, it was deeply entrenched.

And then, after Gov. Murkowski appointed her to the Alaska Oil and Gas Conservation Commission, she had come up against the party boss himself, Randy Ruedrich (see chapter 2), and eventually the governor.

Tensions were running high in the Republican party as the primary election drew near, with three candidates running—Palin, Murkowski and John Binkley, a wealthy Fairbanks businessman.

The tension turned into a free-for-all at the annual Republican picnic in early August 2006, where the party's attorney ran afoul of a group of sign-carrying Palin supporters, accusing them of improper campaigning.

According to reports from attendees, which differed, there was some shoving, name-calling and poking (with a campaign sign), with the event culminating in the lawyer's abrupt departure.

"While making clear her philosophical embrace of Republican party issues, she has made it equally clear that she will serve Alaskans—all Alaskans—and not just the interests of party leaders. Anyone who pays the slightest attention to the political scene at any level knows that talk is cheap on the campaign trail. But in blazing this new path, Palin has already shown she is capable of walking the walk, too," her hometown newspaper, the Mat-Su Valley Frontiersman, wrote on Oct. 17, 2005, a day before Palin announced she would run against Murkowski.

Rep. Eric Croft, an Anchorage Democrat and also a 2006 candidate for governor, called Palin a "bright and honest" person who would be a popular candidate.

"Sarah has been a leader in trying to restore ethical government to Alaska. I think that's badly needed. I think Sarah is very popular with the rank-and-file Republicans, she's just unpopular with the corrupt leadership they have. I hope she doesn't let their antagonism stop her from cleaning up her party."

Palin announced her candidacy on Oct. 18, Alaska Day, saying it was "time to take a stand and put Alaska first."

Palin ran for lieutenant governor in 2002

Sarah Palin first ran for statewide office in 2002—at the request of U.S. Sen. Frank Murkowski, R-Alaska, who was running for governor. (In Alaska candidates for lieutenant governor and governor run separately until after the primary.)

All three of the other Republican candidates for lieutenant governor were better known than Palin, who was a former two-term mayor and council member from the small town of Wasilla, north of Anchorage.

The other candidates were former House Speaker Gail Phillips, considered by many the early favorite; state Senate Majority Leader Loren Leman; and veteran state Sen. Robin Taylor. All three had raised more than triple the $49,000 Palin brought in for her campaign.

She presented herself as a breath of fresh air, an outsider with no ties to special interests and big money, with executive experience.

It didn't hurt that Palin was visually attractive, her 2002 campaign manager Judy Patrick told Petroleum News in September 2008. Patrick was a professional photographer and had an advertising agency in Anchorage. She was also one of Palin's two closest friends.

"When you have a very low budget, you use the assets you have," said Patrick. The two met when Palin was elected mayor of Wasilla for the first time and Patrick was serving on the Wasilla City Council.

Private polls were leaked to the press, showing Palin close behind Leman, who was in the lead.

But days before the August 2002 primary election, anonymous copies of court records showing a 1993 fishing permit violation of Palin's as a felony were sent to reporters. The records were incorrect. The violation was not a felony.

As the results came in on election night Palin was running neck-to-neck with Leman until the results from rural precincts came in that gave him a 1,962-vote win.

Palin campaigned for the Murkowski and Leman ticket.

Murkowski talks about signing gas line contract

Political "theater" at its finest began when Murkowski, ousted in the Aug. 22, 2006 primary election, vowed to continue to push his fiscal contract for a natural gas pipeline to Canada in the time he had left in office.

"It's the only game in town," he said of his deal with BP, ConocoPhillips and ExxonMobil.

Murkowski said he would call the Legislature back into session once the pipeline deal had been revised and would ask lawmakers to approve it. He would leave office in early December.

That prospect did not sit well with some legislators, or with Palin.

She preferred a project by the Alaska Gasline Port Authority that would run alongside the trans-Alaska oil pipeline from the North Slope to the Port of Valdez, where the gas would be liquefied and shipped to the West Coast on tankers, although she also said that as governor she would be willing to consider other pipeline proposals, and promised an open and transparent process.

While Murkowski did not say he would definitely sign the gas line fiscal contract, he didn't rule it out.

In early November, the Alaska Legislature filed a lawsuit to enjoin Murkowski from signing the contract without approval by the Legislature.

The Superior Court granted the Legislature's request for a restraining order on Nov. 9.

Murkowski filed a petition for review before the Alaska Supreme Court on Nov. 14.

The state's high court denied that petition.

Palin, Democrat Knowles and independent candidate Andrew Halcro all said the lawmakers had done the right thing.

"The Legislature, I respect the action they took," Palin said.

Won without much party support

In 2006, when she was running to unseat then-Gov. Murkowski

in the Republican primary, Palin got a call from Ben Stevens, then president of the Republican-run Alaska Senate and son of U.S. Sen. Ted Stevens, R-Alaska.

"He told me, 'You're not just running against Murkowski. You're running against me, my dad, the whole state Republican Party,'" Palin told the Wall Street Journal two years later.

He wasn't kidding.

According to the Alaska Public Offices Commission, Palin received only $5,500 in campaign funds from the state Republican Party for her race against Knowles in the general election.

But Palin did benefit from advertising by the Republican Governors Association, and she received $20,000 of in-kind services from the party and tens of thousands from local Republican districts and women's groups.

In the last week of the race, as the percentage points were closing between her and Knowles, who raised at least $200,000 more than she did and spent most of it in the general election race, Dittman said of Palin's increasing popularity, "Alaska's pretty close to turning a page politically, and she's part of the new leadership."

Probably the biggest change from her own party has come from out-going state senator and fellow Republican, Lyda Green, who in late September 2008 stopped making vitriolic comments about Palin to the press.

And from Ruedrich who handed his McCain-Palin campaign sign to Palin for an autograph at the end of her farewell rally Sept. 13, 2008, in Anchorage.

How much will a gas line cost?

How much will a gas pipeline cost to build from Alaska's North Slope to Lower 48 markets?

That depends on whether you build it all the way to Chicago or stop in Alberta, Canada, where an existing pipeline system is expected to have the capacity to take it to Lower 48 markets.

The cost estimates have increased as the price of materials, such as steel, and labor have gone up.

As of Sept. 29, 2008, the cost of the project, including the portion from Alberta to the U.S. Midwest was expected to hit $30 billion, per an e-mail Petroleum News received from Scott Jepsen, the Denali project's gas line external affairs manager.

The estimate, Jepsen said, is based upon prior work performed by Denali's owners, BP and ConocoPhillips.

Denali's focus between now and the start of open season in 2010 is to update the cost of the project, he said.

Reprint from Jan. 20, 2008, Petroleum News

Good news for Alaska

Study expects 42 percent unused space in gas lines out of Alberta, B.C. by 2018

By Gary Park
For Petroleum News

A natural gas pipeline from Alaska to Lower 48 markets holds the key to heading off a looming plight for the five export pipelines

A GLANCE FORWARD

out of Western Canada, which could face 42 percent unused capacity by 2018, says a new study by the Canadian Energy Research Institute.

In a capacity outlook for Western Canada's pipeline system, CERI suggests that using the spare capacity on both TransCanada and other export systems would require "significantly less contractual commitments" from shippers and offer toll savings compared with expansion of the Alliance pipeline from British Columbia to Chicago.

CERI said unused take-away capacity out of Western Canada is currently 2.5 billion cubic feet per day or 83 percent utilization and could increase to 3.5 bcf per day or 74 percent utilization in 2012 and 6.9 bcf per day or 58 percent utilization in 2018.

The current export capacity from Alberta and British Columbia, to Canada, the U.S. Midcontinent, New England, Mid-Atlantic states, and California and the Pacific Northwest is 14.98 bcf per day.

That includes 7.21 bcf per day on the TransCanada system, 2.77 bcf per day on Gas Transmission (owned by TransCanada), 2.18 bcf per day on the Foothills-Northern Border system (owned by TransCanada and ONEOK Partners), 1.63 bcf per day on the Alliance pipeline and 1.1 bcf per day on the Duke Gas system.

CERI said gas production in Western Canada "keeps going at near-record levels, despite operating at times like a rapidly quickening treadmill.

"And there's plenty more to come down the pipe—from Canada's Mackenzie-Beaufort basins, Alaska's North Slope and Canada's High Arctic."

Oil sands expected to consume more natural gas

But the leading forecasters—CERI, the National Energy Board and Alberta's Energy Conservation Board—agree there will be a significant increase in gas consumption in the Alberta oil sands, which CERI predicts could rise from 1 bcf per day to 6 bcf per day.

Coupled with a decline in conventional gas output, that would result in reduced deliveries to all Alberta export lines, except the Alliance system, the report said.

In addition, development of coalbed methane, LNG imports to Western Canada through Kitimat, British Columbia, and new deliveries from the Mackenzie Delta would add to supply availability, although these developments would be unlikely to reverse the declining trend, the researcher suggested.

Multiple markets for Alaska

CERI said shippers from Alaska would have access to multiple markets in North America, utilizing the existing infrastructure out of Alberta and beyond.

"It is difficult to quantify the value of access to multiple markets, but these connections would allow shippers to optimize floe direction, market deliveries, and, ultimately, product value," CERI said.

Utilizing spare capacity on TransCanada's Alberta system and associated export pipelines "would not only mean significantly less contractual commitments from the Alaska shippers, because of the minimal facility requirements, but would also offer the Alaskan shippers a 20-30 cent per thousand cubic toll saving compared with the Alliance expansion."

The study said the same toll saving would be realized by current shippers from the Western Canada Sedimentary basin to eastern markets.

CERI estimated an Alaska Highway pipeline would cost C$14.5 billion for the Alaska section and C$16.4 billion for the Yukon-British Columbia portion.

Tariff estimated at $2.69 per mcf

The combined average transportation tariff for gas from Prudhoe Bay to Boundary Lake, Alberta, could be $2.69 per thousand cubic feet, assuming 4.5 bcf per day delivered to Boundary Lake.

The report estimated that carrying Alaska gas to Chicago on the Alliance pipeline would need C$2.6 billion for a connector pipe within Alberta and C$11 billion for incremental pipe and compression facilities along the entire system.

That would translate into a combined average transportation tariff from Boundary Lake to the Chicago area of US$1.61 per thousand cubic feet, CERI said.

In contrast, transporting Alaska gas to Chicago via TransCanada and Foothills-Northern Border pipelines could require C$1.8 billion for additional pipe and compression facilities, all of them in Alberta, resulting in a transportation tariff of C$1.30 per thousand cubic feet.

Peter Howard, CERI's senior research director, told the Globe and Mail that "all things being equal, if the flows in the pipelines (from Western Canada) continue to decline then at some point in time it would be a concern for the pipeline companies and for the producers indirectly."

Should the result be higher tolls that would further erode the economics of Western Canada's costly gas industry, he said.

Reprint from the March 9, 2008, Petroleum News.
Clark was the man who headed Gov. Frank Murkowski's gas line
team in its negotiations with the North Slope producers.

Murkowski chief of staff pleads guilty to fraud

According to his plea bargain, Clark will assist
feds in Alaska corruption probe, giving fuel
to rumors of more indictments to come

**By The Associated Press
& Petroleum News**

Jim Clark—the man who represented former Alaska Gov. Frank Murkowski at the gas line negotiating table with ExxonMobil, BP and ConocoPhillips—has pleaded

A GLANCE FORWARD

guilty to federal fraud charges. Clark, chief of staff for the former governor, told a federal judge March 4 that he hid more than $68,000 in campaign payments from state regulators.

The money came from Alaska-based VECO Corp., an oilfield service firm that lobbied heavily for both Gov. Frank Murkowski's petroleum production tax legislation and the gas pipeline contract negotiated for the state by Murkowski with the three North Slope producers, BP, ConocoPhillips and ExxonMobil.

In exchange for the illegal payments, the criminal division of the U.S. Department of Justice said, "Clark used his official position and the Office of the Governor to continue advocating for important oil and gas legislation, that Clark knew was supported by VECO and its corporate executives.

Jim Clark

Considered the most powerful non-elected person in Alaska's state Capitol when Murkowski was governor, Clark told reporters that the former governor never knew of his sleight-of-hand deals to hide campaign contributions from state regulators.

"He trusted me to do things the right way, and I didn't," he said.

It's quite a fall for Clark, a man never afraid to wield his extensive political clout to his advantage, but now he is ensnared in a wide-ranging federal corruption probe that has also touched state and federal lawmakers.

Clark issued apology

About 10 hours before Clark entered his plea March 4, he e-mailed The Associated Press a statement, in which he apologized six times.

"It is ethically and morally wrong for a public official to violate Alaska's laws under any circumstance," Clark wrote. "I should have drawn a line between my job and the campaign and simply left fundraising to the campaign fundraisers. No one is more aware of my inappropriate conduct than I am. For this I sincerely apologize to all Alaskans."

The letter's tone comes in stark contrast to the confident, polished man who spent four years walking the halls of the Capitol in

Juneau doing much of the heavy lifting for Murkowski, and who was referred to not-so-jokingly as "Gov. Clark.".

Clark never minced words, said current and former lawmakers. Nor was he afraid to interrupt a House floor session by ringing Speaker John Harris' podium phone.

Those kinds of calls are rare, but not unheard of. They don't come from Gov. Sarah Palin's administration, Harris said, but he added Clark's calls didn't change the course of any bill.

The news of Clark's plea jarred memories of the man's take-charge style that some say found him beholden to the powerful oil industry as well as loyal to his boss and longtime friend Murkowski.

Remembered for bullying tactics

Former Democratic House Minority Leader Ethan Berkowitz, who served while Murkowski was in office, called the news tragic, but says he can't forget what he called four years of bullying tactics.

"There was an unholy alliance of big oil, the Murkowski administration and the Republican operatives that treated the Legislature and state assets as their own private domain," said Berkowitz, who is now running for Congress.

"They operated by threat instead of logic," Berkowitz said. "You do better with people by persuading them, than when you try to bully them, but that's what he did."

Berkowitz said Clark once told lawmakers that if they didn't pass a statewide sales tax, there would have to be cuts in social programs. And the hubris didn't stop there, Berkowitz said. Even against the Legislature's wishes, Murkowski bought a jet on the state's dime so he could travel around Alaska and to the Lower 48 more quickly.

"Jim Clark told the Legislature what was what; the level of arrogance was astounding," Berkowitz said. "They were out of touch with the whole machinery of government."

Clark, who also is an attorney, led the Murkowski administration in negotiations with the three North Slope oil producers on fiscal terms with hopes of getting a gas pipeline built from the North

Slope to Lower-48 states' markets.

VECO executives Bill Allen and Rick Smith stood to benefit from a gas line project and courted a handful of lawmakers to advocate for industry-friendly legislation. VECO was the oil field services company founded by Allen, which vigorously promoted the position of the North Slope producers in Juneau.

The gas line contract negotiated by Clark was not approved by the Alaska Legislature.

Both Allen and Smith pleaded guilty to federal charges last year for bribing Alaska lawmakers in the ongoing federal investigation, which also has touched U.S. Sen. Ted Stevens, the longest serving Republican in the Senate.

Stevens is being investigated for a remodeling project at his home in Girdwood, a ski resort community on Anchorage's southern edge. Allen has testified that he sent VECO employees to work on the house.

Beyond saying he's paid every bill presented him for the remodeling project, Stevens will not comment on the investigation.

U.S. Rep. Don Young, R-Alaska, is also the subject of a federal investigation that includes his campaign finance practices. Young's re-election campaign last year spent $854,053 on legal fees, but he won't disclose for what that money was used. Neither has been charged. ....

Read the rest of the story online at:
www.petroleumnews.com/pnads/338810902.shtml

Department of Natural Resources Commissioner Tom Irwin had been scheduled to attend a press conference with Gov. Frank Murkowski on the gas line fiscal contract with the three North Slope producers and said he'd been told that, if he was a team player, he was going to start telling the public that the fiscal contract was a good deal. Irwin said he couldn't do it; "I'll work internally, but I cannot tell the Alaska public it's a good deal; and I won't," he said of his 2005 decision.

Chapter 4

The gas line: a new start

"Explorers are not going to risk exploration capital in Alaska" without "access to the gas line."

—Gov. Sarah Palin, December 2006

By Kristen Nelson

I t had been the pot of gold at the end of Alaska's energy rainbow for 30 years: a gas pipeline from the North Slope to markets in the Lower 48 states.

In recent years, with declining crude oil production reducing the state's revenues and rising natural gas prices making a gas pipeline look more feasible, the State of Alaska had tried to find a way to get a gas project moving, a way to motivate the huge capital expenditures required for a project estimated to cost as much as $25 billion.

Alaska's newly elected Gov. Sarah Palin highlighted her interest in getting a gas line started by spending the two days following her Dec. 4, 2006, inauguration in discussions with potential gas pipeline sponsors and shippers.

How the state could—or should—encourage a natural gas pipeline had been a central issue in the 2006 Alaska gubernatorial race.

The administration of Frank Murkowski—Palin defeated him in the Republican primary in August 2006—spent months trying to get legislative approval for a fiscal-terms contract it negotiated under the state's Stranded Gas Development Act. That contract would have given gas owners the stability on tax and royalty issues which proponents of a line said they required.

Plus a whole lot more, a charge which became public in the fall of 2005 when senior Department of Natural Resources officials were fired or quit because they believed the contract gave too much

What are sponsors and shippers?

"Sponsors" and "shippers" are terms that occur in Alaska gas pipeline discussions. A sponsor is a company with ownership in a pipeline or proposing to have ownership in a line; a shipper is a company that has a contract to move its gas through the line.

The North Slope producers, Alaska's Big 3 oil companies—BP, ConocoPhillips and ExxonMobil—planned to be both sponsors of the line and shippers on the line. Other companies, such as Anadarko Petroleum, planned to ship on the line once they discovered natural gas.

to the North Slope's three natural gas leaseholders and only major oil producers—BP, ConocoPhillips and ExxonMobil.

The Alaska Legislature spent the late spring and summer of 2006 being briefed and holding hearings on the Murkowski contract, but it never came to a vote, although legislators did pass a revision to the state's oil and gas production tax, viewed as step one of the contract approval process.

Palin's opponent in the November 2006 general election, Democrat Tony Knowles, who was governor from 1994-2002, ran on opening the negotiation process to more companies, while Palin ran on establishing a different process for the state to support gas pipeline development, one she described as more open, transparent and competitive.

The competition angle

After her election in November 2006 Palin started to build a gas line team.

Since she wanted to encourage competition for a gas line, she invited potential gas line sponsors and shippers to a series of meetings Dec. 5-6.

The meetings were introductory sessions with a dozen companies and organizations:

• The Big 3 North Slope oil producers, the leaseholders that had proven gas reserves and owned controlling interest in more than 90

Rutherford understands constitutional rights

Alaska Gov. Sarah Palin named Marty Rutherford acting commissioner of the Department of Natural Resources Nov. 28, 2006—one of the first three commissioners the newly elected governor named. Palin said Rutherford "understands constitutional rights," and said Rutherford would join her at post-inauguration talks with companies interested in seeing a gas pipeline built to take North Slope gas to market.

Rutherford, then 55, had been DNR deputy com-
missioner for more than 10 years for both Democratic
and Republican governors. She was one of six depart-
ment officials who resigned after Gov. Frank
Murkowski fired DNR Commissioner Tom Irwin in
October 2005 because Irwin objected to the way in
which a contract was being negotiated with Alaska's
North Slope oil producers—BP, ConocoPhillips and
ExxonMobil—under the Alaska Stranded Gas
Development Act.

Marty Rutherford

DNR lost seven officials, dubbed "The Magnificent Seven" from the movie title by DNR employees, over concessions the Murkowski administration was making in the fiscal contract negotiations (see chapter 2).

Under the Murkowski administration Rutherford was lead negotiator on a preliminary gas line contract between the State of Alaska and TransCanada, one of the alternative pipeline sponsors Murkowski set aside when he decided to focus on reaching a deal with the three North Slope producers, who collectively held the majority of the North Slope's proven reserves of 35 trillion cubic feet of natural gas.

As to the interim nature of the appointment, Rutherford originally took leave from a job at the Alaska Mental Health Trust Land Office to come on board as commissioner.

"I'm excited to do this and help while I can, and we'll see how things evolve," she said when named to the post. Rutherford said she was looking forward to returning to DNR and the gas line issue. "It's been a year or so since I've been involved," she said in late November 2006. "I'm looking forward to participating next week in discussions with explorers and produc-
ers." When Tom Irwin returned as DNR commissioner in February 2007, Rutherford returned to her deputy commissioner slot; she continued to lead the Palin administration's gas team in 2008.

Oil tanker receiving terminal at Port of Valdez in Southcentral Alaska. The 800-mile trans-Alaska oil pipeline starts at Prudhoe Bay on the North Slope and terminates here.

percent of northern Alaska oil production facilities and pipelines;

• Explorers, the oil and gas companies with gas-prone acreage and mostly estimated gas reserves, but no controlling interest in existing production and pipeline infrastructure;

• Gas distribution and pipeline companies that own no oil and gas production; and

• The two public bodies established to focus on in-state and liquefied natural gas projects.

State officials at the meetings included the governor, Lt. Gov. Sean Parnell, Commissioner of Revenue Pat Galvin, Acting Commissioner of DNR Marty Rutherford and Kurt Gibson of DNR's division of oil and gas.

Rutherford had been part of gas line negotiations under Murkowski and was one of the six senior DNR officials to quit after Murkowski fired DNR Commissioner Tom Irwin in October 2005.

Galvin had been in DNR's division of oil and gas under Murkowski, and his appointment as Revenue commissioner was a step in ensuring those two departments would work together more successfully under Palin than they had under Murkowski or previous governors.

The governor believed the Stranded Gas Development Act needed to be replaced and said it was her intention to introduce a "law of general application and allow that competitive atmosphere that I think we need to be in, in order to get the best project."

Palin said a bill, to be introduced when the Alaska State Legislature met in early 2007, would "provide for all proposals to be considered in a more open, competitive manner."

The stranded gas act was premised on confidential negotiations between the state and potential project sponsors, or owners. The Murkowski administration received multiple proposals under that statutory authority, but ended up focusing on a single project, a proposal by the major North Slope oil and gas producers for a pipeline project to the Lower 48 through Canada, a project in which the state would take an equity (ownership) share.

Fiscal certainty still an issue

Palin said after the December meetings that she was pleased by the enthusiasm of many of the participants and by their ideas for commercializing the state's gas.

One thing she heard was the "need to see the Legislature onboard with the administration, working as a team for Alaska, in order to progress this project."

The governor said fiscal certainty was brought up in the meetings. "Obviously the producers themselves would like to see fiscal certainty," she said, referring to BP, ConocoPhillips and ExxonMobil.

Another thing the administration heard was "that explorers are not going to risk exploration capital in Alaska" without "access to the gas line," Palin said.

Rutherford said the access issue was "a very significant difference" between the Big 3 producers, with proven and ready-to-develop gas, and explorers, with gas prospects that would take longer to put into production.

Explorers also said they needed a reasonable tariff and the certainty that the line would be expanded when their gas came online.

The explorers weren't necessarily interested in being project sponsors (owners), Rutherford said, but were interested in knowing there would be opportunities to explore and then to get gas from any discoveries that they made onto a pipeline.

Palin said one thing that stuck with her from the meetings—in addition to the need to have the Legislature onboard—"was that unreasonable timelines and expectations will not get us a gas line. That was a lesson learned," she said, and confirmed for her that "artificial timelines" are not productive.

"We don't want to, again, raise some false hopes in terms of timelines here," the governor said, "but it's a doable project and I think the state would be very wise to continue down this path of inviting all interested participants to give us their input."

Rutherford said those at the meetings didn't see any window for Alaska natural gas closing abruptly, and "virtually every party continued to say this is a very economic project" because, even though the cost of labor and steel was on the rise, so were natural gas prices.

The group did not get to that same level of discussion about the economics of the project and whether a window was closing with the major North Slope producers. The producers are "still very enthusiastic about this project so that would indicate to me they still think it's an economic project, but they ... want a lot of state assistance to move the project forward," Rutherford said.

Palin had been supportive of the Alaska Gasline Port Authority's liquefied natural gas project out of Valdez, and the port authority was one of the groups meeting with the governor and her gas line

Irwin, Palin saw eye-to-eye on environment

Tom Irwin, Gov. Sarah Palin's commissioner of Natural Resources, was fired from the same post in October 2005 by then Gov. Frank Murkowski when Irwin refused to go along with how the Murkowski administration was negotiating a gas pipeline deal.

Irwin subsequently supported Palin in her run for governor, headed up her transition team for the Department of Natural Resources and joined the Palin administration as DNR commissioner in February 2007.

Tom Irwin

Irwin was ousted by Murkowski after he wrote a memo in October 2005 to then-Alaska Attorney General David Marquez, asking for legal advice on whether the Murkowski administration was acting within its authority under the Stranded Gas Development Act in its negotiations with the North Slope producers—BP, ConocoPhillips and ExxonMobil.

Irwin copied Murkowski and the governor's chief of staff, Jim Clark, on that memo.

Irwin said in a 2008 interview that he was asking for legal advice from the Department of Law, a request that falls under client-attorney privilege. Irwin said he copied Murkowski and Clark because he always copies the boss.

Marty Rutherford, then—as now—a DNR deputy commissioner, was in the room when he e-mailed the memo and they agreed that was one memo that would "never see the light of day."

Irwin said he still doesn't understand why Murkowski made the memo public.

Irwin had been scheduled to attend a press conference with Murkowski on the fiscal contract and said he'd been told that, if he was a team player, he was going to start telling the public that the fiscal contract was a good deal. Irwin said he couldn't do it; "I'll work internally, but I cannot tell the Alaska public it's a good deal; and I won't," he said of his 2005 decision.

When Murkowski read the Oct. 20 memo he put Irwin on administrative leave and then released the memo.

Irwin said he doesn't know why the memo was distributed: "Did they just want an excuse to get rid of us? Did they want to challenge

continued on page 69

A CLOSER LOOK

Galvin took a stand on Point Thomson

Pat Galvin, formerly a section chief in the Department of Natural Resources division of oil and gas, was named commissioner of Revenue by incoming Gov. Sarah Palin Dec. 1, 2006.

Galvin, then 41, was a petroleum land manager in the division of oil and gas and chief of the oil and gas leasing and permitting sections. Prior to moving to the division, Galvin was director of the division of governmental coordination which manages the Alaska Coastal Management Program. Its successor, the division of coastal and ocean management, is part of DNR.

Kevin Banks

Pat Galvin

Galvin, along with division of oil and gas section chiefs Kevin Banks of commercial (Palin later appointed Banks acting division director) and Julie Houle of resource evaluation, recommended that ExxonMobil's 2006 Point Thomson development proposal be rejected and the unit put into default, a recommendation in which the three were unanimously supported by their staffs.

Mike Menge

This was when Mike Menge, named by Murkowski to replace Irwin, was making a decision on whether to concur with former division of oil and gas director Mark Myers and terminate the Point Thomson unit, based on the failure of unit operator ExxonMobil to submit an acceptable plan of development.

Mark Myers

The three said the plan "should be rejected because it does not commit the PTU owners to timely development and production" from the unit and "offers even less to that end than the rejected" 2005 plan. The new plan also did not contain any of the requirements of the 2005 decision which rejected the earlier plan, such as "specific commitments to timely delineate the hydrocarbons (drill wells) underlying the PTU and develop the unitized substances."

Irwin: A combination of things...

what we were doing?" Irwin said he doesn't know, but he's wondered a lot about it.

As to why Irwin didn't join the Palin team when the governor was elected, Irwin said it was a combination of things.

First, his wife was recovering from an accident in their home—their grandson's dog jumped up unexpectedly, whipping his wife's feet out from under her. Her arm was outstretched, he said, and the result was a shattered ball in her shoulder and a broken arm. She couldn't lie down for almost two months, had to sleep sitting up: "I was not going to leave her," Irwin said.

The other reason he didn't immediately accept Palin's offer was that he wanted to be sure he could work with this governor, having "learned that it can be miserable—you need to know, really know, who you're going to work for."

Palin initially caught Irwin's attention after he was fired when, on principle, she left a six-figure job at the Alaska Oil and Gas Conservation Commission (see chapter 3).

He and Palin started having conversations "along the lines of somebody's got to stand up for Alaskans," Irwin said.

During her run for governor, Irwin talked to her about "non-confidential gas issues" and how the system worked, and endorsed her bid for governor.

Palin asked Irwin to come back as DNR commissioner after the election, but his wife was still recovering and he wanted to make sure he and the governor agreed on the fundamentals so that the governor wouldn't be put in a position of having to fire him—and he wouldn't be put in a position of having to quit.

Irwin said he and Palin are on the same page with resource development and the environment: pro-resource development, but not at the expense of hurting the environment.

And Irwin also wanted to hire his own team, irrespective of party affiliation. He'd wanted to hire Nan Thompson when Murkowski was governor, but wasn't allowed to because Thompson had prominent Democratic friends.

Irwin didn't care about Thompson's political connections. He wanted to hire her because "she's one of the best lease attorneys in the state" and he needed her in DNR. Palin said she wouldn't interfere with Irwin's hiring decisions and Nan Thompson was one of the first people he hired.

team. Palin said it was great to talk with the port authority and that her "assurance to them is that they are on that level playing field along with everyone else, without a bias towards or against them."

What went wrong?

Asked what participants in the meetings said about the Murkowski process under the Stranded Gas Development Act, Palin said some "felt that there was some confusion with what it was that the administration was driving toward in the negotiations."

And some of the companies interested in building a gas line "didn't know if they were being seriously considered ... or if they were, I guess speaking bluntly here, if they were just being used as leverage in negotiations with the big three oil companies."

Palin said she assured participants that the goal of her administration was to act with honestly and transparency and that "we would not treat them that way—that we will not lead them on, in terms of being allowed to participate early on without the intention of seriously and fairly considering their proposals."

Rutherford said that concern was expressed by everybody in the meetings except the three North Slope producers.

The producers have argued that they are the only ones with the wherewithal to do such a project, but Palin disagreed, saying some of the large pipeline companies have strong capital positions and needed to be seriously considered.

Palin direction different

Palin had been clear that she was moving away from the Stranded Gas Development Act.

"I trust that all the participants know that that's what our intention is." It was also "to introduce that law of general application and allow that competitive atmosphere that I think we need to be in, in order to get the best project," she said after the meetings.

Galvin, talking about those meetings a year and a half later, recalled all of the North Slope producers telling the governor individually that she needed to start with the Stranded Gas Development Act.

He said the meetings with the North Slope producers provided a "clear indication that the election itself was not going to change their position, even though she had campaigned against the stranded gas contract, said that it was not the way she was going to go. They came in basically saying, 'hey, you've got to start with the stranded gas contract.'"

The governor told the companies she did not want to go with the existing stranded gas act process, but the North Slope producers said that was where the administration needed to start.

Rutherford said her recollection was that the meetings were reflective of who the companies were. BG, for example, a major gas company in an exploration partnership with Anadarko Petroleum and Petro-Canada, said it was concerned about open access on a gas pipeline for explorers.

The North Slope producers—BP, ConocoPhillips and ExxonMobil—were concerned about fiscal certainty, wanting to know in advance what the state's tax and royalty take would be. Rutherford also said, speaking about the meetings in September 2008, that it was implicit that for the three North Slope majors everything on the table under the Stranded Gas Development Act was still necessary.

There was no give from the producers, she said.

Major players return

Palin wanted a fresh start on reaching a gas pipeline deal, but she benefitted from a body of knowledge that had been built up over the years on gas pipeline issues.

When the Alaska Legislature convened in January 2007, many legislators and staff, as well as state employees, had backgrounds in gas pipeline issues gained in the Murkowski administration and, in some cases, the Knowles administration.

Palin had invited key players in the earlier contract negotiations who were fired or quit in protest over the Murkowski contract with the Big 3 to join her administration.

Before she was inaugurated, Palin had named Rutherford, who would lead her gas line team, as acting commissioner of Natural Resources.

Rutherford was one of the DNR officials who quit in 2005 after then DNR Commissioner Tom Irwin was fired.

Irwin headed up Palin's transition team for DNR and later joined the administration in February 2006, at which time Rutherford reclaimed the deputy commissioner slot she had held for 10 years.

Revenue Commissioner Pat Galvin had been a DNR manager under the previous two governors. He said in a 2008 interview that one issue discussed when the governor talked to him before his appointment was the value of having a better relationship and more cooperation between the departments of Revenue and Natural Resources.

*Reprint from the Dec. 24, 2006 issue of Petroleum News. This
article will give readers an idea of the kind of dialogue that took place
in the early December 2006 meetings between newly elected Gov. Sarah
Palin and her gas pipeline team with potential gas line shippers and
sponsors, as well as a glimpse into the status of a North Slope LNG
project, something Palin had touted in her campaign for governor.*

What role for ANGDA under Gov. Palin?

New governor asks agency to take another look at LNG project in voter initiative, but not pushing that as number one for state

By Kristen Nelson
Petroleum News

Why hasn't the Alaska Natural Gas Development Authority pursued an LNG project out of Valdez?

Apparently it was a question Gov. Sarah Palin asked ANGDA CEO Harold Heinze, board Vice Chairman Scott Heyworth and board member Dan Sullivan when they met with the governor, the lieutenant governor and leaders of the Palin gas team in early December 2006.

Pat Galvin

As Commissioner of Revenue Pat Galvin put it when the ANGDA board discussed it at a Dec. 18 meeting, the governor's reaction seemed to be that it was great the authority was pursuing a spur line to Southcentral, but wasn't ANGDA "intended to be bigger than that?" Galvin said the governor considers herself answerable to the public and she wants to go back and recognize what was in the initiative voters approved.

"You identified a more focused agenda," he said, and the governor would like an explanation of how the board identified its role as the spur line. Perhaps it was a reaction to the previous administration, Galvin said, and suggested the board might want to "take the opportunity with this new administration to go back and look at that question again before we proceed with a particular view of what ANGDA's role in all this is going to be."

FORREST CRANE

Harold Heinze

Heinze said he felt the Palin administration "was asking ANGDA to go back and take a harder look at a project that makes sense within the State of Alaska," something he said he would call "an Alaska-market-based project."

ANGDA has looked at what it called a "bullet line"—a backup position in the event that a main line taking gas through Canada is not built. Heinze said such a project would need to include both Cook Inlet and Valdez, and said he thought the administration was "looking to us to bring forward some information at some point that sort of defines what the opportunity was there, what the project might look like."

Heinze said he certainly didn't get the impression this was the first or second choice of the group, but was something "the administration wanted on the list and wanted to understand enough about."

If a project into Southcentral is considered, "Valdez is an essential component of it," Heinze said. The market that exists in Southcentral is "so small that the economics of all this become very difficult. If you include Valdez, even at very modest volumes, it has a significant lowering of cost of service to this area."

Murkowski administration 'very cool'

The main emphasis of that initiative was a Valdez-based LNG

project, although as Heyworth—the initiative sponsor—told the board, while the words in the initiative describe a gas pipeline from Prudhoe Bay to tidewater at Prince William Sound, he did include a spur line through Glennallen in the initiative.

He said it was wonderful to be received by the governor and her staff, and said he thought it would be "very helpful to the governor" to look at ANGDA as the "vehicle for in-state gas."

Heyworth noted that Marty Rutherford, acting commissioner of the Department of Natural Resources, was looking at a "smaller in-state project that cracks North Slope gas open."

FORREST CRANE

As for the ANGDA focus under the Murkowski administration, "We picked up what we could do," he said, and lived to fight another day.

ANGDA board Chairman Andy Warwick con-curred, characterizing the Murkowski administration

Scott Heyworth

as "very cool" toward an all-Alaska gas pipeline project (i.e. gas to Valdez for LNG). He also said the Alaska Gasline Port Authority, which is pushing a Valdez-based LNG project, "was pursuing it very aggressively and acquired access to permits," so it was "counterpro-ductive to compete with the port authority."

However, Warwick said, "Gov. Palin would have significant influ-ence over who took that project on—probably she would be the determining factor." The effort to put together an all-Alaska gas proj-ect would be "monumental," he added, for whichever entity the administration backed.

ANGDA never lost track of LNG

Heinze said ANGDA has "never lost track of the LNG idea." The authority knows a little more about alternatives than it did, he said, and "if you look back through the reports you'll see that a lot of what we did is usable under a very wide range of circumstances."

And, he said, ANGDA has "maintained a good relationship with those type of people that we believe that if we got gas to tidewater, they would come and build the LNG plant, build the ships, haul the gas off—and we wouldn't even have to make those investments."

Heyworth noted the memorandum of understanding ANGDA has with Mitsubishi and said both he and Heinze have worked to keep that relationship alive, to keep that option open.

Heinze said he took the opportunity to pitch the spur line and LNG from Valdez to another potential player when BG was in town to talk to the governor about the North Slope gas line project. There are five mega oil companies, he said, "there is only one mega gas company—British Gas." (Editor's note: the company now goes by "BG".)

BG became involved in North Slope exploration prospects early in 2006 as a partner with Anadarko Petroleum and Petro-Canada in the Brooks Range Foothills and later in the year in partnership with Anadarko in acreage including Jacob's Ladder south of Badami.

Heinze said he pitched BG over lunch.

"They are one of the two or three or four people in the world that would have a large interest in building an LNG plant and the tankers and developing the market—if we got the gas to tidewater. They're also the kind of people that might be willing to go upstream of that point," he said.

Heinze said BG is probably the largest player in LNG shipments, and called it an interesting connection that was possible because the governor threw open the door to people to come make their pitches. ...

Read the rest of the story online at:
http://www.petroleumnews.com/pnads/109882199.shtml

"It's time to leave the Stranded Gas Development Act in the past and move forward with a new vehicle. A vehicle that builds on the knowledge and experience gained from a valiant—but futile—effort previously in a noncompetitive process."

—Gov. Sarah Palin, January 2007, state-of-the-state address

Chapter 5

AGIA: Palin proposes new way forward

The ... Alaska Gasline Inducement Act ... would be "transparent and competitive" and would jumpstart the process using incentives, while striking "the right balance on a project for the state, the nation, project proponents and producers."

—Gov. Sarah Palin, January 2007, state-of-the-state address

By Kristen Nelson

Alaskans got a pretty good idea of what Sarah Palin had in mind for natural gas development while she was running for governor in 2006.

She expanded on those ideas in her first state-of-the-state address to the Alaska Legislature in January 2007.

Palin's direction hadn't changed—it was away from the Stranded Gas Development Act the previous administration used to try to jumpstart a gas pipeline project.

She had made her distrust of Murkowski's stranded gas negotiations clear during the campaign, siding with Department of Natural Resources officials who repudiated Murkowski's contract in the fall of 2005 and saying she would hire them.

Gov. Sarah Palin

And she did. By February 2007 she had DNR Commissioner Tom Irwin and DNR deputy commissioners Marty Rutherford and Dick LeFevre back on board.

In an opinion piece published in the Mat-Su Valley Frontiersman in June 2006, during the gubernatorial campaign, Palin said that to know which alternative for North Slope gas development most benefits the state required allowing "all viable entities to compete for the right to tap our resources and progress this project sensibly and legally."

When asked by the Anchorage Daily News how her administration would move forward on a natural gas pipeline and how her plan compared with the proposal negotiated by the Murkowski administration, she said that all qualified proposals would be considered.

"The Stranded Gas Development Act no longer applies. We will introduce a bill seeking a 'law of general application.' The bill will set forth key requirements, such as access to gas for Alaska communities, jobs for Alaskans, pre-construction benchmarks, expansion provisions, reasonable tariff structure and legislative approval. The bill will also set forth incentives to qualified applicants that guarantee quick commencement," Palin said.

Competition—along with transparency and a good public process—were central to the Palin administration gas line proposal.

North Slope gas not stranded

Alaskans learned a lot from attempts by the Murkowski administration to develop the state's North Slope gas under the stranded gas act.

What they primarily learned, Palin told legislators in her January 2007 state-of-the-state address, was that "Alaska's gas isn't stranded." The reason for the stranded gas act was the belief that it would be too costly to get North Slope gas to market without assistance— that it was stranded by the lack of a gas pipeline, the cost of building that pipeline and the low price of gas in the Lower 48 states— and because the gas was stranded, the state needed to provide cuts in its taxes to make the project economic.

While there were still risks, the governor said the project no longer needed the kind of tax cuts and other assistance envisioned in the fiscal contract negotiated by the Murkowski administration.

"While bringing natural gas to market is costly and risky, there's no question this is a sound, economic project," the governor said.

Palin said the state also learned that North Slope producers would talk to the state under the stranded gas act, "and talk to us, and talk to us until we agree to their terms."

Terms proposed by the Big 3 North Slope producers—BP, ConocoPhillips and ExxonMobil—included giving up some of Alaska's fundamental rights as a state, "because the deal removed our taxing, regulatory and judicial authorities for decades," she said.

The state needs progress on a gas pipeline, she said, and it needs competition.

"It's time to leave the Stranded Gas Development Act in the past and move forward with a new vehicle. A vehicle that builds on the knowledge and experience gained from a valiant—but futile—effort previously in a noncompetitive process," she said.

AGIA under development

The new way forward was to be contained in an administration bill entitled the Alaska Gasline Inducement Act, or AGIA, a bill that would induce construction of a gas pipeline built on the state's terms.

The process would be "transparent and competitive" and would jumpstart the process using incentives, while striking "the right balance on a project for the state, the nation, project proponents and producers," Palin told legislators.

Later in January 2007, in remarks to the Alaska Support Industry Alliance's annual conference in Anchorage, the governor said that in addition to inducements for a gas pipeline builder, and an opportunity to compete for the inducement package, AGIA would provide inducements to those who hold the leases and control the gas to encourage them to commit gas to an AGIA project.

She acknowledged that AGIA was "an unprecedented approach," and said "that's what leadership, new ideas and new energy are all about."

AGIA was devised in the administration's first month, Palin said, and was being evaluated by experts. While she'd originally hoped to put AGIA in the hands of the Legislature on the first day of the session in mid-January, the governor said the administration would continue to work on the bill until it was satisfied it would pass legislative and public scrutiny and attract applications from qualified sponsors.

Legislative focus on gas

Leadership in the Alaska Legislature, which had spent a good part of 2006 on a natural gas pipeline proposal and a related tax bill, said at the beginning of the session that a gas line would be a big item on the agenda for 2007.

Sen. Charlie Huggins

Sen. Charlie Huggins, R-Wasilla, chair of Senate Resources, said in mid-January as the session got under way that Alaskans had made it clear a gas pipeline was their first priority. Gov. Palin has created a high expectation in the state for a gas line, he said, "and it's our job to be part of delivering that as a separate and equal body of our government."

As for changes from the 2006 stranded gas process, Huggins said he thought "Alaskans expect a more public process."

Rep. Ralph Samuels

But, he said, there was a window of opportunity and "we have to meet that window of opportunity."

House Majority Leader Ralph Samuels, R-Anchorage, said he thought the gas line was "the issue" for both the minority and the majority. He

Rep. Mike Chenault

said he planned some background briefings on gas issues while the administration completed work on its bill, since there were new members and not all of the returning members had "lived and breathed" the gas line issue in 2006.

Rep. Mike Chenault, R-Nikiski, co-chair of the House Finance Committee said he thought it was imperative that the state move forward on a gas line.

"I don't believe that we can sit around and wait three or four years to make a decision on a gas line," he said, adding he expected the Legislature to work with the governor and provide information to the administration to move the process along.

AGIA: Vetting by experts

Marty Rutherford, head of the governor's gas team and in January 2006 still acting commissioner of Natural Resources, said the goal behind the administration's in-depth review of AGIA by experts was to ensure that the gas line legislation was a "fully fleshed approach" and was "commercially reasonable," resulting in "a project moving forward in a very specific fashion."

To do that, the administration was reaching out to people in specific gas-pipeline-related professions for their opinions, as well as getting feedback from potential applicants on the overall approach.

"I've asked that this not be put in the Legislature's hands, for their consideration, until we have absolute confidence that this is going to result in a project," Palin said at a press conference in mid-January.

Rutherford said a crucial difference between AGIA and the stranded gas act was that AGIA would specify what the administration believed Alaska should receive from a gas pipeline project. A reasonable tariff was one of those things; an assured process for expansion of the line as new gas was found was another, she said.

Palin said what differentiated AGIA was that under the stranded gas process "we just never knew what the benchmarks were on behalf of the state, what were those must haves, what were those components that we couldn't live without."

"It seemed to be so evolving all the time and we would find out after the fact that a concession was going to be provided to the producers."

The governor said that would be different in AGIA: "We want to lay out, from the start ... what these components are that we can't live without to make sure that Alaska's interests are being met."

The administration also got feedback on its proposals from the companies and organizations the governor met with in December, including the North Slope producers and major pipelines.

The governor emphasized the reasons for AGIA in a weekly gas update in early February. The old stranded gas act, she said, "requires a finding (a determination by state officials) that the gas is stranded. Our gas is not stranded."

Palin said that for the gas to be stranded, "its value must be insufficient to support a free market pipeline."

But independent legal, commercial and engineering consultants have agreed, she said, "that the current and expected value of the gas is sufficient" to make a project commercial.

Two other important differences in AGIA, she said, were that it was a competitive process, which the stranded gas process was not, and AGIA established what the state needed for the gas line project to work, which the stranded gas process had not.

The governor said her gas team was meeting with experts. "I'm discussing the gas line with federal officials and its significance to the nation," she said, and working on ways the federal government could help get the line built.

National gas issues

When the administration rolled out AGIA at the beginning of March, the governor highlighted the national perspective, telling an audience of oil and gas company and state officials that she had just returned from Washington, D.C., "where I had the opportunity to discuss the Alaska gas line and the critical role that Alaska plays in our national energy policy and the role that we can play in a national security plan."

The nation was watching Alaska's gas line actions, the governor said.

"I listened to the president talk about his concern regarding America's dependence on foreign oil and I don't know if you see it, but I see and am fearful of our nation headed down the same path with gas.

"And that's unacceptable. Alaska can and must help," Palin said.

"I think we should all agree that we cannot afford to allow clean, safe, domestic energy supplies to sit untapped any longer. ... As I discussed our AGIA plan with federal officials, it was confirmed that with energy, Alaska's interests are really the same as the nation's interests.

"We all want a gas pipeline to move forward as expeditiously as possible; we want low tariffs; we want an open-access line so that new fields will be explored and new reserves developed and shipped through the line for decades to come."

$500 million

The governor said the state was telling project proponents up front what it was offering: "a state matching capital contribution for the cost of obtaining that initial regulatory certificate to build. It sounds like a jaw-dropping figure—up to $500 million that the state would be offering," she said, about half of the estimated cost to get a certificate for the project from the Federal Energy Regulatory Commission or the Regulatory Commission of Alaska, depending on the project. This would be state matching monies for work advancing the project.

The proposed Murkowski fiscal contract would have cost the state $13 billion to $14 billion, "plus unquantifiable value of our resource development future," the governor said.

In AGIA the state's contribution was "on the table for all to see" and would be "our real skin in the game here that proves our commitment." That amount will be returned to the state, "over and over again through the years, in the form of those lower tariffs which results in higher royalties from production."

AGIA designed to move gas line forward

Irwin said he was privileged to be standing with the governor and the gas team as AGIA was rolled out.

"AGIA moves the gas line forward. We're confident of that. ... The state is now in control of moving the process instead of standing by and waiting." With the fair, open process in AGIA, the gas project "is no longer high centered," he said.

Irwin said he kept hearing that Alaska was so close to closing the deal struck by Murkowski with the producers and all that was needed when Palin came into office was to tweak it.

"Wrong. There is no other completed deal," he said, noting that the limited liability company language in the Murkowski contract was never completed. "If the originators of that deal can't agree on even who's the leadership, the LLC language is not complete. This state cannot and will not jeopardize all judicial rights, legislative rights and various administrative rights for up to 45 years for an option contract," Irwin said, referring to the fact that the Murkowski fiscal contract only committed the North Slope producers—BP, ConocoPhillips and ExxonMobil—to do due diligence on a line.

AGIA incentives included $500 million in matching funds, a pipeline coordinator to oversee permitting and a training program so that Alaskans will be prepared for pipeline construction jobs, said Commissioner of Revenue Pat Galvin.

On the gas resource side the incentives included royalty issues and production tax, he said. The royalty inducements for producers who made a commitment to the initial open season for an AGIA-licensed project included protection from the higher-of provision in royalties—the state evaluation of all royalty sales which required sellers to retroactively match the highest price received for any of the state's gas.

The state's ability to switch from taking its royalty gas in kind or in value would also be limited, Galvin said. And the tax rate in place at the time of the open season would be the tax rate paid for the first 10 years of gas flow; a taxpayer committing gas in the initial binding open season would be exempt from any tax increases over the rate in place at the time of the open season for the first 10 years of gas shipment.

Galvin said a low tariff would be supported by debt-to-equity ratio requirements.

He said AGIA also contained provisions for expandability—a requirement that the pipeline owner solicit for shipping requirements and commit to expand when there was demand.

Feds embrace AGIA

FERC Chairman Joesph Kelliher

Rutherford said Alaska's congressional delegation, FERC Chairman Joseph Kelliher and U.S. Department of the Interior Secretary Samuel Bodman, all "embraced the AGIA requirements that ensure that the Alaska gas pipeline project will be an open-access pipeline."

Interior Secretary Samuel Bodman

The congressional delegation, FERC, the Regulatory Commission of Alaska and oil and gas companies exploring on the North Slope, all "recognize that an open-access pipeline is the only means of ensuring that Alaska's gas flows to the markets for decades to come."

AGIA ensured open access by requiring the pipeline to solicit new gas every two years—and expand to accommodate that gas if there were adequate quantities—and by requiring commitment to a tariff structure that produced the lowest reasonable tariff, Rutherford said.

"The requirements in the AGIA that the gas line project be an open-access pipeline and move forward expeditiously with identified benchmarks were embraced in Washington, D.C.," Rutherford said.

"They understand that Alaska's resources will serve the national and Alaskan energy needs with clean, abundant and secure gas, for decades."

*Reprint from Feb. 18, 2007 Petroleum News. The first pull
in a tug of war between the CEOs of the Big 3 North Slope oil
companies and Alaska's new CEO Sarah Palin.*

Palin parries low blow
from ExxonMobil

G ov. Sarah Palin, in response to disparaging remarks from
ExxonMobil Chairman Rex Tillerson Feb. 13, fired back a day
later with acidic comments of her own.

Tillerson, in discussing what he called access
and contractual challenges in Alaska at the
Cambridge Energy Research Associates conference
in Houston, Texas, told reporters that he didn't
know where things were headed with the gas line
and he didn't think Alaska knew where it wanted
to go, either.

Rex Tillerson

Calling Tillerson's comments "unfortunate,"
Palin said she believes ExxonMobil knows exactly
where Alaska is going with the gas line and doesn't
like that direction.

Gov. Sarah Palin

"What bothers me is that Alaska tried it Exxon's
way," Palin said. "The result was a contract that is
not viable. It did not have the support of the public or the Legislature."

Palin vowed that her administration will continue to pursue a
competitive, open and transparent process to achieve a gas line deal
that will benefit all parties involved.

"It's painfully obvious that ExxonMobil does not want that

Images of Alaska's oil and gas industry

By Judy Patrick

Drilling is drilling

No matter what fancy new techniques come along, drilling is still hard work and roughnecks have to put in a bit of muscle to connect joints of pipe.

Ice road: re-paving arctic style

A water tanker puts a smooth surface on an Alaska North Slope winter ice road. Ice roads are built from water and snow. Water is a great building material in January, but come spring the State of Alaska requires all traffic along the ice roads to cease.

When the ice melts, there is no road left at all.

The tundra is untracked. Scrappy shrubs and flowers flash out to struggle for growth in the short Arctic summer. Living plants greet the eye in places winter's heavy traffic once ruled. When winter returns, it's time for the tankers to lay down the roads again.

In most cases, exploration wells are drilled from ice pads. Ice roads work best near a source of fresh water on terrain that is not too hilly.

Sun kisses Osprey platform on calm Cook Inlet afternoon

The Osprey production platform looms above a flotilla of boats installing an undersea cable from shore. In June 2000, independent Forcenergy installed the Osprey over the Redoubt Shoal field in Cook Inlet.

Innovation delivered the Osprey at a fraction of the cost of conventional platforms, allowing the exploration and development of a hitherto non-commercial 1969 oil field discovery.
In 2008, Long Beach-based Pacific Energy Resources produces oil and gas from the Osprey. The independent plans to drill more wells from the platform.

Workers reach Osprey via a five-minute helicopter ride from Pacific Energy's base near the Kuskatan River. Osprey is a half-hour flight from Anchorage.

Rolligon convoy 2007

A Rolligon—officially an ultra low impact vehicle—has puffy low pressure air bags rather than tires. The vehicles carry up to 85,000 pounds without impacting the Arctic's tundra.

Offshore exploration in the Arctic

The SDC (steel drilling caisson), a bottom-founded Arctic drilling platform, was used to drill the McCovey prospect in the Beaufort Sea, 12.5 miles northeast of West Dock at Prudhoe Bay.

McCovey today is a lonely point on the map, some five miles northeast of Reindeer Island. Calgary-based Alberta Energy, now called EnCana, drilled the prospect in early 2000. The SDC has an air-tight subsea chamber.

McCovey was a bust. No commercial quantities of oil and gas were found. ConocoPhillips and Chevron were partners in the venture.

Heavy cargo; easy does it

Heavy modules are slowly nudged onto BP's Northstar production island. Two process modules weighed in at 3,500 tons and 3,700 tons. The compressor module tipped the scales at 3,500 tons.

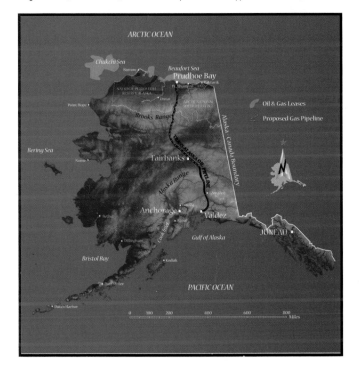

Tanker n' Tugs

The fully laden tanker Polar Alaska is attended by tugs as it steams to sea from Valdez, the southern terminus of the trans-Alaska oil pipeline.

Trans-Alaska oil pipeline

The 800-mile-long trans-Alaska oil pipeline is one of the largest pipeline systems in the world. Starting in Prudhoe Bay on Alaska's North Slope, the pipeline snakes through rugged and scenic terrain to Valdez—the northernmost ice-free port in North America.

The pipeline started up in 1977. At a cost of almost $8 billion, it was the largest privately funded construction project at that time.

The 48-inch diameter pipeline crosses three mountain ranges and more than 800 rivers and streams.

North to Northstar; plying the Arctic Ocean

A 2001 sealift to BP's Northstar oil field development project included two process modules, a compressor module, a pump skid and a warehouse/shop building. The modules were fabricated in Anchorage.

process. We know exactly where we're going and have a plan to move forward. Exxon doesn't like that plan because it puts the interests of Alaska and the nation, first—and not Exxon."

Palin said she plans to introduce the Alaska Gasline Inducement Act in the state Legislature in about two weeks, and looks forward to continuing positive dialogue with everyone interested in moving the gas line forward and bringing Alaska's gas to market.

She also said she plans to meet with ExxonMobil in Washington, D.C., within two weeks and "hopefully, we can get to the bottom of this."

"It's unfortunate that the top dogs at Exxon would come out swinging. They haven't seen AGIA. I think it's very premature. ... I would prefer a much more positive relationship with a company involved in the process and not one that is so adversarial, right off the bat," she added.

—Rose Ragsdale

"In my personal belief, we have gone from being in front of the curve to being in back of the curve right now."

—Joe Marushack, vice president of gas development for ConocoPhillips Alaska, February 2007

Chapter 6

AGIA a step backward for Big 3

"Prices go up, prices go down: We have the impact. Costs go up: We have the impact. The only time the pipeline company is really at any risk is for those dollars between when the project's planning starts and when a successful open season is met."

—Joe Marushack, vice president of gas development for ConocoPhillips Alaska, February 2007

By Kristen Nelson

How did the North Slope producers react to AGIA? Polite but restrained at the governor's Alaska Gasline Inducement Act announcement in early March, the companies who through leases own the majority of the known gas reserves on Alaska's North Slope—BP, ConocoPhillips and ExxonMobil—had spent the previous administration arguing that a gas pipeline was not economic and required state assistance.

They pursued this view with Gov. Palin at her introductory gas line meetings in early December.

The new governor's view that a gas pipeline project was economic and therefore North Slope gas was not stranded was the view that had been championed by opponents of the fiscal contract the companies negotiated with the Murkowski administration.

Marty Rutherford, the head of Palin's gas line team, was one of the Department of Natural Resources officials who quit in 2005 after DNR Commissioner Tom Irwin was fired by Murkowski over disagreements with that administration's gas pipeline negotiations. Irwin returned as DNR commissioner under the Palin administration in early February 2007.

Palin had run for governor opposing the Murkowski gas pipeline contract.

The new administration was clearly taking a different direction than the plan laid out by the Murkowski administration and the North Slope producers.

Gas pipeline timing issues

Speaking to legislative committees in February 2007, before the Alaska Gasline Inducement Act was released, but when its broad outlines were well known, the producers outlined what they saw as important issues in moving a gas line forward.

"In my personal belief, we have gone from being in front of the curve to being in back of the curve right now," Joe Marushack, vice president of gas development for ConocoPhillips Alaska told the Alaska Legislature's Senate Resources Committee early in February 2007. Marushack, who was getting ready to leave Alaska to take over ConocoPhillips' Australia business unit, said he regretted not getting the gas pipeline moving in the six years he spent in Alaska.

Joe Marushack,
ConocoPhillips

And he raised the specter of the window to get Alaska gas to market starting to close.

Marushack said he believed "now more than ever, that we're at a critical time in moving this project forward." He said he hadn't believed there was a limited window for getting Alaska's natural gas into the Lower 48 market because with natural decline in U.S. and Canadian production there would be a need for North Slope gas. About two years ago things had started to change, with "growing competition, not only of gas-on-gas, but of all the other energy sources out there" and "massive competition for critical components" needed for a gas pipeline—steel, machinery, labor, technical engineering and project management.

Energy competition was coming from coal-fired plants which were being permitted in areas like Texas that traditionally hadn't burned coal for power. Once coal was chosen for a new power plant, that fuel would be burned for 30 to 50 years, reducing the market for natural gas, Marushack said. Liquefied natural gas, LNG, was also a competitor, with gas coming into the U.S. from other parts of the world.

The markets need to know that Alaska gas is coming, before other competitive fuel sources are selected, he said.

Had the contract negotiated last year been finalized, "this project could be moving forward. We would be hiring Alaskans and moving it forward today as we speak."

With a new process proposed by the Palin administration it would take time to bring people up to speed. When ConocoPhillips brings new people in on the Alaska gas project, people who already have 10 to 15 years experience in gas, it still takes them a year to come up to speed because moving Alaska natural gas is a complicated and massive project, Marushack said.

"So I think it's going to take a new Legislature and a new administration a certain period of time to really get comfortable with the issues and be able to move it forward."

Resource issue critical

Marushack said what needed to be addressed before a line could be built were issues around the resource—i.e. natural gas.

"If we can address the resource issue, the pipeline falls out of that." That is critical because the resource "pays for everything through the shipping commitment," he said, referring to what is called the "ship-or-pay" commitment that prospective shippers sign before a line is built.

Once a company proposing a pipeline has binding commitments to ship gas, those commitments become the basis for obtaining financing to build the pipeline. That's because the tariff for shipping on the pipeline pays the bills: It pays for operating costs, but more importantly, it pays back the cost of building the line.

While more gas is expected to be found and shipped on the line, there are already some 35 trillion cubic feet of known gas on the North Slope, on leases primarily held by BP, ConocoPhillips and

What is ship or pay?

Before a gas pipeline is built, prospective shippers commit to ship gas on that line for a period of time, providing the backing for the pipeline builder to obtain financing for the line.

"Ship-or-pay" is a commitment to ship gas, whether or not gas is available to ship on a particular day.

A shipper on a gas pipeline pays for a volume allocation on the pipeline, and signs a contract to pay for that volume allocation even if the shipper doesn't have gas for the line. That is why explorers—companies that do not yet have proven reserves of natural gas on the North Slope—are hesitant to commit in advance of discovery and development: If a discovery doesn't prove to have enough gas to be an economic development, or if development takes longer than projected, that shipper may be paying for space on a pipeline without gas sales to support that payment.

Ship-or-pay commitments are made following an open season, when the prospective pipeline builder lays out expected costs and tariffs and invites potential shippers to commit volumes to the pipeline.

ExxonMobil. The long-term shipping commitments for the line, Marushack told legislators, would be "based on the balance sheets and the resources of the three major North Slope producers," and the state, which owns a royalty share of the gas.

"Those producers and the State of Alaska basically are going to pay for this project," he said.

When shippers make a ship-or-pay commitment, they commit to pay the tariff—whether they have gas or not on a given day and irrespective of the price they get for the gas in the market.

A proposed gas pipeline from Alaska's North Slope failed in the late 1970s and early 1980s because the price for gas in Lower 48 markets dropped—and estimates to build the line rose—to the point where shippers would have received less for their gas than they paid in a tariff to ship it.

Reserves a plus

Marushack pointed out to legislators that the state was in the same position as the companies because if the cost of building the pipeline was more than expected, the state would get less tax revenue, since that revenue was based on the value of the gas at the well—i.e. the price received in the market less transportation costs.

That transportation cost, the pipeline tariff, would be based on what it cost to build and operate the gas line.

The state and the producers "share a huge amount of risk on this project and that's really another reason why I believe we should be aligned in moving it forward," he said.

That was in contrast to the pipeline owner, which would receive a regulated rate of return based on its equity contribution.

If the cost of building and operating the pipeline went up, the pipeline owner would transfer that cost hike to the shippers. The shippers would bear the risk of the price in the market and they bear the risk of the cost of the pipeline, Marushack said.

"Prices go up, prices go down: We have the impact. Costs go up: We have the impact," he said. "The only time the pipeline company is really at any risk is for those dollars between when the project's planning starts and when a successful open season is met," he said, arguing that once a pipeline had signed ship-or-pay commitments in hand—at the end of a successful open season when the project was sanctioned—it would borrow money to proceed and that money would be paid back by shippers through the tariff.

Arguing against the matching money the state was proposing to put in as part of AGIA, Marushack said upfront costs were relatively small, perhaps $400 million to $1 billion to get to project sanction, compared to the total cost of $20 billion to $30 billion. If a firm couldn't fund that upfront cost of $400 million to $1 billion, the gas line project probably wasn't one they should be taking on, he said.

Reaction to proposals

Marushack said the issues that needed to be resolved included reaching agreement on how the producers would be taxed and what the royalty terms would be "so the producers can make this massive shipping commitment and be relatively certain that any potential value and upside is simply not going to be taxed away over time."

Under the agreement the producers had reached with the Murkowski administration, he said, "the producers will take a lot of the risks inherent in a major mega project, but we ask your understanding and your help in addressing issues that really are under your control."

Speaking in early February 2007—AGIA wasn't released until early March—Marushack said the producers didn't have all the details, but believed "splitting the pipeline issues from the resources issues—and I believe that is going to be part of the proposal based on what I've heard so far—has some merit."

The pipeline issues were "actually pretty simple," and you work those one way. The resources issues "which are actually very complicated" are worked another way, he said.

"I also think the idea of looking at different pipeline proposals makes some sense for the state ... but I really think that the fundamental issue remains you have to address the resource side of the equation. If you're successful on the resource side, the pipeline will fall out of that."

Mega size of gas line an issue

Marushack said he was frustrated by discussions of the pipeline as though it were a parking garage: You've built them all over the place, just scale it up and you've got a big parking garage.

The proposed North Slope gas pipeline "is nothing like Lower 48 pipelines. This is a major infrastructure project, on scale with anything in the world," he said.

"And as such there are really no models for this project. It's unique.

"It's got a myriad of complexities and there are very few simplifications that you can make in this project."

You can get caught in an endless loop of what-ifs, he said, and you never get to the finish line on the project.

What's necessary is to focus on the most critical issue, Marushack said: "The most critical issue is getting started on the project right now."

Once you get started on the main project, other things fall in place. "If you want a spur line into Southcentral (Alaska), that spur line is a lot more economic if it's built off of this major, economy-of-scale main pipeline project. If you want to take liquids off, again, you're a lot better off taking liquids off an economic, massive project than any other concept that I can think of."

An economic project would create jobs in the state, he said, and if the pipeline were coming, "we would be exploring for gas and that's a whole new massive industry for the State of Alaska."

And it's to the advantage of the producers that the project is successful and "spins off substantial revenue to the state, because we need additional sources of revenue ... and this gas pipeline should provide that."

The emotional issues

Marushack said there are issues that become emotional.

One of those is fiscal certainty.

"I suspect when producers say fiscal certainty some people think that's an attack on self-sovereignty. It's really not, but some people think it is," he said referring to the desire on the part of the producers to know what the tax rate on the project will be out into the future, typically described by the companies as the same length of time for which they would make ship-or-pay commitments on the pipeline.

From the producers' side the emotional issue is rolled-in rates, he said. (Rolled-in rates are tariffs for pipeline expansions which are the same for original shippers and shippers on the expansion capacity; this is standard in Canada but not in the United States.) "When folks say rolled-in rate, I can tell you we think that's code for subsidizing other companies."

Both, he said, are areas where the companies and the state need to "work our way through and not be caught up in that rhetoric."

"I honestly believe ConocoPhillips and the state are aligned in wanting to have the best project ... move forward. We want revenues for the state and we want revenues for ourselves. We want an exploration business here. We want to grow this business. We think we have a lot of insight into this area and probably some competitive advantages. And we want this project to happen."

The economic issue

Marushack said there was also a misunderstanding around how economic a gas pipeline project would be.

"There's a misunderstanding this project is wildly economic—obviously economic."

Nobody could really say that, he said in February 2007.

The companies had put $125 million into a cost estimate in 2001 and had come up with $20 billion for a line from the North Slope to Chicago.

"Since then, steel prices have doubled; labor's gone way up; the queue for equipment has drastically changed; project management skills are much more difficult to find. And the bottom line is nobody, not us, not anybody else," can provide an estimate on the cost "until they rebuild all that engineering work. Now I can tell you it's not $20 billion anymore," he said; probably more like $25 billion. (See Petroleum News reprint at the end of this chapter.)

Marushack said it would take about $100 million to get to a better cost number.

The gas price market was volatile, he said, and "nobody really knows what prices are going to be" a decade or more in the future when gas begins to flow.

ConocoPhillips was ready to work with the Palin administration and the Legislature to move the project forward. "I don't see any way you can move this forward if we're not actively engaging together," Marushack said.

He said again that addressing resource issues was the key to addressing the pipeline, and that the state had to "provide adequate security to the companies in the areas where the state can, so that those shipping commitments can be made, because they're the critical component in making this project happen." The gas pipeline would serve a lot of parties, he said, but the producers and the state were the ones that would be on the hook for the project.

Open season issues

Getting the gas into a non-producer pipeline was a concern for legislators if the Big 3 companies were not willing to sell it.

Sen. Bert Stedman, R-Ketchikan, asked Marushack what the key issue would be to ensure that the producers would show up to commit their gas in an open season.

Marushack said the first thing that would be needed was "to have some sort of agreement with the state on just what the true-ups are going to be on taxes."

Sen. Bert Stedman

Comparing a shipping commitment to a house where the producers were going to live in the house and make payments on the house, "we've got to know that we're going to have the wherewithal to pay for that house and to actually make some profits when we do that. So I believe we've got to have a deal around the fiscal terms that will allow those shipping commitments to happen."

He also said that if the shippers were basically paying for the house, they wouldn't want to pay a rate of return to somebody else when they could own the house as well as pay for it, and pay that rate of return to themselves.

Cost overruns on the pipeline were also an issue, he said. If ConocoPhillips were to build the gas pipeline, the company would have ownership and "we'll take the cost overrun risk." It's something the company has done all over the world, he said.

If someone else built the gas line "they wouldn't have the same interest in making absolutely guaranteed that it's the lowest cost project," Marushack said.

The producers were interested in managing the cost—and that meant matching up throughput with ownership, i.e. a company whose gas filled 20 percent of the line would expect to own 20 percent of the line.

An open season with no commitments of gas "would be a terrible thing for the state; it would not be a good thing for the producers." It would cost time and send "a terrible signal to the market" and could result in litigation with more potential for delay, he said.

Senate Resources Chairman Charlie Huggins, R-Wasilla, asked if there were showstoppers Marushack hadn't touched on.

Marushack said resource issues—fiscal certainty—had to be addressed, along with the rolled-in tariff issue.

And, he said, "I personally have trouble figuring out how you make that shipping commitment if you don't control the cost."

Other North Slope producers concur

While Marushack took the lead in this round of testimony, the first hearings involving the producers under the Palin administration, others concurred.

ExxonMobil's Martin "Marty" Massey, the company's U.S. joint interest manager, compared the gas pipeline to major international projects. It is "a basin-opening project, and with any basin-opening project, it requires alignment between the host government and the leaseholders," he said.

To finance such a project required "strong sponsors with proven track records and the financial strength to act upon commitment," commitment in the form of firm transportation (ship-or-pay) agreements. Financial institutions would require "long-term ship-or-pay contracts ... by creditworthy parties who may not elect to continue ownership of the pipeline after construction is done and the pipeline is in place and gas is being shipped," he said, suggesting that producer owners of a gas pipeline might stay on board to ensure that costs were controlled and then sell their interests in the line.

On alignment with the state, Massey said in response to a question from Stedman that if the producers and the state were at odds, "then you know we're not going to be successful."

In the Murkowski deal, "we were aligned in that we both had ownership positions in the project," so both had money in the deal. The state didn't have to take an equity share, he said, "but it has been a concept that has been proven successful in many projects around the world for the host government ... to take an ownership in a big project."

Risks for a pipeline company owning the line would be at open season: "Is there somebody there that will actually make a commitment to that project? Once they have that commitment then pretty much, because it's a regulated activity, they're guaranteed a return."

Sen. Bill Wielechowski

Massey said the state would probably find few companies willing to put a lot of money up front until there was a firm transportation commitment.

Sen. Bill Wielechowski, D-Anchorage, asked both Marushack and Massey whether one producer at Prudhoe Bay could participate in an open season without concurrence of the others.

Massey concurred with Marushack, that it was not something the companies had talked about.

"The three of us have said that for a project of this magnitude" it would take "all three of us, including the state."

Some risks borne by producers

Dave Van Tuyl, BP's gas commercialization manager in Alaska, said BP remained interested in getting Alaska's gas to market. Alaska gas represented the largest known undeveloped resource in BP's portfolio, and in addition to the importance of gas production, producing that gas "also extends the economic life of light oil production on the North Slope."

"BP stands ready to work with the new administration and the

Legislature to reach a balanced framework that works for all the parties," Van Tuyl said.

BP saw three risks in the project: price risk in the market, cost risk in building the pipeline, and fiscal and regulatory risk.

"Price is set by markets and we are price takers, not price makers, as resource owners," Van Tuyl said. As for project costs, "as energy prices have increased over the last few years, the costs to bring that energy to market have also risen and they've risen dramatically." Steel prices have doubled, and the project will require millions of tons of steel; labor, fabrication, engineering, permitting and buying equipment were other costs that had increased significantly, he said.

Dave Van Tuyl, BP

Then there were the fiscal risks associated with any project.

Who would bear those risks?

Van Tuyl said price risk was borne by gas resource owners—the Big 3 producers and the state.

The same was true for pipeline cost risk.

"The people that hold that risk, the cost risk, need to be able to manage that risk: They're the ones most incentivized to manage that," he said.

Companies like the North Slope producers were well acquainted with managing project cost risk—they did it "through rigorous project management processes."

"Fiscal risk is mitigated, simply put, by an investor knowing the rules. That's what reduces the investment risk. And the state can work with investors to minimize that risk."

Van Tuyl said BP saw the project moving forward "through an open process that's available to any project sponsor ... with the same rules for ... any party."

He emphasized "allowing the free market to work: That's where the best ideas are created, and certainly a project like this needs good ideas to allow that best project to emerge."

Focus needed to be on "maximizing the value of the resource," Van Tuyl said.

The open season question

Asked by Stedman what can be done to ensure there is a successful open season, Van Tuyl said offering a transportation service responsive to customers (gas shippers) was one key for a successful open season.

That meant "a low-cost project that ... encourages shippers to participate." He said shippers needed confidence that a low-cost project could be delivered, which required confidence in cost management.

Then potential shippers needed confidence "that they know the rules," which meant that resource terms were defined in advance of an open season. "That reduces a huge risk for the resource owners who will be making that commitment," he said.

Huggins asked what parameters might have changed for BP since the extensive fiscal contract talk with the Murkowski administration.

Van Tuyl said BP thought the fiscal contract developed with Murkowski presented a solution to the problems of getting a gas pipeline project moving.

There were questions and issues raised and BP was ready to address those, he said, and was open to new ideas on things like "how best to get the risk and reward balance right. We don't think we have the market cornered on good ideas, and that's why we need to have an open process, get them out on the table and see if we can't find a solution that works for everybody."

Reprint from Jan. 20, 2008 Petroleum News. In 2008 the Big 3 North Slope producers were estimating it would cost $30 billion to build a gas pipeline from Alaska's North Slope to Chicago, but because of excess capacity in the existing pipeline system from Alberta, Canada, to Chicago and elsewhere in the Lower 48 states, the North Slope gas line would cost considerably less if it only had to go into Alberta—probably in the neighborhood of $20 billion, Petroleum News sources said Sept. 29, 2008.

Good news for Alaska

Study expects 42% unused space in gas lines out of Alberta, B.C. by 2018

By Gary Park
For Petroleum News

A natural gas pipeline from Alaska to Lower 48 markets holds the key to heading off a looming plight for the five export pipelines out of Western Canada, which could face 42 percent unused capacity by 2018, says a new study by the Canadian Energy Research Institute.

In a capacity outlook for Western Canada's pipeline system, CERI suggests that using the spare capacity on both TransCanada and other export systems would require "significantly less contractual commitments" from shippers and offer toll savings compared with expansion of the Alliance pipeline from British Columbia to Chicago.

CERI said unused takeaway capacity out of Western Canada is currently 2.5 billion cubic feet per day or 83 percent utilization and could increase to 3.5 bcf per day or 74 percent utilization in 2012 and 6.9 bcf per day or 58 percent utilization in 2018.

The current export capacity from Alberta and British Columbia, Canada, to the U.S. Midcontinent, New England, Mid-Atlantic states and California and the Pacific Northwest is 14.98 bcf per day.

That includes 7.21 bcf per day on the TransCanada system, 2.77 bcf per day on Gas Transmission (owned by TransCanada), 2.18 bcf per day on the Foothills-Northern Border system (owned by TransCanada and ONEOK Partners), 1.63 bcf per day on the Alliance pipeline and 1.1 bcf per day on the Duke Gas system.

CERI said gas production in Western Canada "keeps going at near-record levels, despite operating at times like a rapidly quickening treadmill.

"And there's plenty more to come down the pipe—from Canada's Mackenzie-Beaufort basins, Alaska's North Slope and Canada's High Arctic."

Oil sands expected to consume more natural gas

But the leading forecasters—CERI, the National Energy Board and Alberta's Energy Conservation Board—agree there will be a significant increase in gas consumption in the Alberta oil sands, which CERI predicts could rise from 1 bcf per day to 6 bcf per day.

Coupled with a decline in conventional gas output, that would result in reduced deliveries to all Alberta export lines, except the Alliance system, the report said.

In addition, development of coalbed methane, LNG imports to Western Canada through Kitimat, British Columbia, and new deliveries from the Mackenzie Delta would add to supply availability, although these developments would be unlikely to reverse the declining trend, the researcher suggested.

Multiple markets for Alaska

CERI said shippers from Alaska would have access to multiple markets in North America, utilizing the existing infrastructure out of Alberta and beyond.

"It is difficult to quantify the value of access to multiple markets, but these connections would allow shippers to optimize floe direction, market deliveries, and, ultimately, product value," CERI said.

Utilizing spare capacity on TransCanada's Alberta system and associated export pipelines "would not only mean significantly less contractual commitments from the Alaska shippers, because of the minimal facility requirements, but would also offer the Alaskan shippers a 20-30 cent per thousand cubic toll saving compared with the Alliance expansion."

The study said the same toll saving would be realized by current shippers from the Western Canada Sedimentary basin to eastern markets.

CERI estimated an Alaska Highway pipeline would cost C$14.5 billion for the Alaska section and C$16.4 billion for the Yukon-British Columbia portion.

Tariff estimated at $2.69 per mcf

The combined average transportation tariff for gas from Prudhoe Bay to Boundary Lake, Alberta, could be $2.69 per thousand cubic feet, assuming 4.5 bcf per day delivered to Boundary Lake.

The report estimated that carrying Alaska gas to Chicago on the Alliance pipeline would need C$2.6 billion for a connector pipe within Alberta and C$11 billion for incremental pipe and compression facilities along the entire system.

That would translate into a combined average transportation tariff from Boundary Lake to the Chicago area of US$1.61 per thousand cubic feet, CERI said.

In contrast, transporting Alaska gas to Chicago via TransCanada and Foothills-Northern Border pipelines could require C$1.8 billion for additional pipe and compression facilities, all of them in Alberta, resulting in a transportation tariff of C$1.30 per thousand cubic feet.

Peter Howard, CERI's senior research director, told the Globe and Mail that "all things being equal, if the flows in the pipelines (from Western Canada) continue to decline then at some point in time it would be a concern for the pipeline companies and for the producers indirectly."

Should the result be higher tolls that would further erode the economics of Western Canada's costly gas industry, he said.

"From our perspective, the negotiations conducted by the previous administration under the stranded gas act were not fruitful for many reasons. ... (AGIA) is a positive step towards revitalizing the gas pipeline development process in a way that will move the project forward."

—Kirk Morgan, Kern River Gas Transmission Co., part of Warren Buffet's MidAmerican Energy Holdings Co.

Chapter 7

What role for the pipeline companies?

AGIA is also an attempt to clearly state the question to the producers: "Will you sell your gas at a certain price? Or will you accept a certain tariff rate and agree to commit your gas?"

—Commissioner Pat Galvin, Alaska Department of Revenue

By Kristen Nelson

It wasn't just the North Slope producers who were interested in an Alaska gas pipeline project.

So were independent pipelines, particularly Enbridge, Kern River and TransCanada.

Pipeline companies were interested in the project because they build pipelines and could build this one, but also because they make money moving gas and Alaska natural gas could add to volumes the companies already move in North America, helping to keep existing lines full.

All three companies talked to the Alaska Legislature in 2007, although only one, TransCanada, ultimately submitted an application under the Alaska Gasline Inducement Act, AGIA.

"We're an unbiased third party" as far as Alaska's issues with the producers are concerned, Enbridge's vice president for gas transmission and development, Doug Krenze, told the Alaska Legislature's House Resources committee in mid-March 2007.

The company has some downstream pipes Alaska gas could ultimately flow through, Krenze said, "But our concern is what it's going to do to the bigger picture long term for the industry." Krenze said that there had been two warm winters and people had forgotten how fragile the natural gas supply-demand was in North America, "extremely fragile," he said.

House Resources Committee Co-Chair Carl Gatto, R-Palmer,

asked about the dual 36-inch lines Enbridge had once proposed from the North Slope.

Ron Brintnell, director of gas pipeline development for Enbridge, said that in 2004 Enbridge looked at dual 36-inch lines. "At that time, the feeling was that it was unlikely the market would be ready for, or able to handle, 4.5 bcf a day out of the chute," he said. Enbridge thought if it built a 36-inch line initially it could ramp up gas deliveries over time and then build a second line as needed.

Rep. Carl Gatto

Since needs had increased over time, the market should be able to take a full 4.5 billion cubic feet a day. "The reality is, the market's more than ready for it now," Brintnell said.

On the subject of producer ownership of a line, Krenze said it's a control issue. "Let's be honest, they, the producers, will bear the risk on this pipeline; they have to, you have to have them contract for the capacity of the pipeline." Shell developed pipelines in the Gulf of Mexico, he said, because "they wanted to manage the cost, they wanted to manage the timing, they wanted to protect against overruns."

"The producers in this situation are exactly in the same boat with even a bigger, larger project staring them in the face."

Enbridge thinks that for the Alaska pipeline to proceed "the producers have got to play a key role in this project," Krenze said. "And ... we've looked at the AGIA and I think ultimately the intent is that they would come to the table. Our concern is with respect to timing. We would like to see them at the table sooner, rather than later."

The pipeline is a pipeline project, but issues between the state and the producers need to be resolved and once that happens, the pipeline will move forward rapidly, he said.

The creditworthiness of the producers will be important for financing to keep the tariff as low as possible, Krenze said, and based on his experience in the industry he thinks that for the producers "to come to the table and sign up for 35 years ship-or-pay contracts, they're going to want to have control, cost control over the project, because they're going to bear the risk of the cost overruns."

He told legislators that to progress the project, he recommended the state get the producers back to the table, "try to resolve and reach your compromises on the issues that are still to be resolved, because until those compromises and issues are resolved and there is agreement, the pipeline is going nowhere."

If AGIA passes there will be requests for pipelines to submit applications, Krenze said.

"I can tell you, unless we could come together with a producer consortium, we as one of the major North American natural gas companies are not going to spend our time or take the risk to go through this process and then three years after we have a license from Alaska, go to an open season and have nobody commit for any capacity on the open season after we've spent hundreds of millions of dollars."

Tough in open forum

Krenze said he realized "a lot of time and energy and emotion" had been devoted to trying to reach a deal and that the fiscal contract process had ended.

But there was significant progress under the Murkowski administration, he said, adding that he thought it would be difficult to negotiate remaining issues in an open forum.

Rep. David Guttenberg, D-Fairbanks, told Krenze he'd worked all his life in the oil fields.

Rep. David Guttenberg

"You had to come to us with a pipeline deal that was really bad in order for us to reject it. And that's what happened" under the Murkowski administration. Legislators spent the interim between the regular sessions, something like 180 days, getting educated. Then there was a "phenomenal election, which turned a lot of things around." Guttenberg said it "should have been a lesson to the industry, the producers, about the attitudes of the people of this state." People in Fairbanks have significant questions, he said, "and it is a public process from our perspective," with significant issues for Alaskans including sovereignty and Alaska hire.

Krenze said he applauded Guttenberg's comments, and said Enbridge is looking at this as an outsider. "We weren't part of the (Murkowski) negotiation."

He said Enbridge does talk to the producers, asking what the company can do to help get the project moving.

"Because it's just the timing concern—and we don't want to see this thing slide another couple of years. That's our message."

He said he doesn't know whether AGIA is the right approach, but "at the end of the day there's going to have to be resolution with the producers before any pipeline project is going to go ahead."

Krenze urged legislators to resolve the state's issues with the producers sooner rather than later, because once all the parties are aligned the project will start moving.

"This state doesn't need to spend half a billion dollars supporting a pipeline application," he said, referring to the $500 million in matching funds in AGIA. "... Fix the issues and the pipeline will move ahead," he said.

Gatto summarized an Alaskan's view of the project when he said, "Our goal is to make money. We're not a charity. We don't have a future without this pipeline."

"You are trying to maximize value long-term for Alaska: And that's your job, and that's what you should be doing," Krenze said. "Other stakeholders are trying to do exactly the same thing for their stakeholders."

TransCanada's Tony Palmer

Tony Palmer, vice president of Alaska business development for

TransCanada Corp., testified before the Senate Resources Committee in late March 2007.

Like Enbridge, TransCanada believes compromise must be achieved between the North Slope producers and the State of Alaska, Palmer said.

But TransCanada holds rights through Canada, so its message has been that a compromise must include the producers, who hold the gas, the State of Alaska and TransCanada, which has rights to build a line through Canada based on agreements reached between the United States and Canada in the late 1970s when a gas pipeline was first proposed from the North Slope to market.

Tony Palmer, TransCanada

Palmer said the company's decision on whether to submit an application under AGIA would depend on the final AGIA bill and the actual terms of the request for applications.

"At present, we will continue, as we have for many years, to work towards a five-party arrangement with the three ANS (Alaska North Slope) producers, the state and TransCanada to advance the project."

As AGIA was discussed in the Alaska Legislature, TransCanada said it did not think that an applicant should be required to continue beyond a failed open season to pursue a certificate of convenience and necessity from the Federal Energy Regulatory Commission. Palmer told Senate Resources the company believes that in the case an initial open season did not attract sufficient customers to fill the line, TransCanada would want to focus on "obtaining the customers as opposed to doing the engineering and regulatory and legal work to capture a FERC certificate."

"Our preference is clearly to continue to pursue customers ... until those customers or an alternate source of credit is available for a project," he said. Financing for pipelines is based on ship-or-pay commitments made in an open season.

No customers, no credit, no pipeline

Senate Resources Chair Charlie Huggins, R-Wasilla, referred to the Enbridge testimony in House Resources and asked Palmer: "They essentially said: no producers; no pipeline; pretty straightforward about that; do you take any exception to that?"

Palmer said he didn't hear the Enbridge testimony.

"I would ... tell you that no customers; no credit; no pipeline.

"So if there are alternate customers (to the North Slope producers) we would be pleased to accept them; if there are alternate credit (sources) we would be pleased to accept those.

"But at the moment we believe the existing leaseholders, at least at Prudhoe Bay" and Point Thomson, would need to commit their gas for a project to move forward, Palmer said, although he acknowledged there is uncertainty about Point Thomson, which was in litigation in March 2007 and remains in litigation in September 2008.

"... clearly no customers; no credit; no pipe," he said.

Commissioner of Revenue Pat Galvin was asked by Huggins to respond to Palmer's comments on the results of a failed open season, and the AGIA requirement that an applicant commit to proceed beyond a failed open season to obtain a FERC certificate.

Galvin said the administration recognized that "part of the challenge that we all face is that we've got a number of different commercial participants in this who have different positions that they've staked out over the years that represent what they see as the value they bring to the project and that they clearly have an interest in protecting those interests and in maximizing the value that they expect to receive for those."

Recognizing that the project is stalemated, AGIA provided an opportunity for as many players as possible to participate, Galvin said, and to bring new energy to the project, because "we do have a situation where the project just doesn't seem to be advancing given the natural interests of all the parties."

AGIA wasn't intended to provide everything any particular party would want, he said. "We recognize that we're pushing all the parties into places where they may not go otherwise except for the natural competition that is going to be brought to bear."

Commissioner of Natural Resources Tom Irwin told the committee: "The program of moving Alaska's gas to market is high centered and it's high centered where we don't want to be held at the mercy of someone saying we need something undefined."

Sen. Bill Wielechowski, D-Anchorage, said he was concerned that there might be a gap in AGIA, that the state might not be doing enough to encourage communication between parties.

TransCanada said we can't do the project without them, he said. The producers said we can't do the project without them. "And yet there seems to be something missing in AGIA that allows for— incentivizes—the parties to communicate with one another."

Irwin noted that he had, up to a point (when he was fired in October 2005) been involved in the previous negotiations. The committee had an excellent line of questioning earlier, he said, asking the parties what they need.

"We have been asking that question for a few years now: What do you need? We'd like to hear what you need defined instead of these great general terms. ...

"Communications is a two-way street: We're listening but somebody's got to tell us what you need."

Galvin told the committee that the Stranded Gas Development Act was put in place "to foster that kind of communication."

He said Exxon's procedure had been to talk to the state, tell the state what the company needed, talk a little more, and have the state eventually agree to give it to them. The state has had a number of years of that kind of one-way communication, he said.

"What we're lacking is some sense of imperative to reach some form of agreement on moving this project forward."

AGIA is not a hindrance to communication, Galvin said. "What it sets up is an imperative to begin maybe a different level of communication, one that ultimately will lead to action."

The administration believes that what is needed is a sense of moving forward—and more direct communication between the parties.

"Because ultimately what we recognize is the state is not going to solve this issue. The state just doesn't have the ability, unless we go into the Permanent Fund and end up spending all that money on it ourselves, to make this thing (the pipeline) happen on our own," Galvin said.

The state needs the commercial players to come together, Irwin said.

"We know that the producers are going to have a role in this. TransCanada feels they need to have a role in it, and ultimately the participants in this are going to have to decide what their respective roles are going to be," he said.

Galvin said there has been a lot of talk up to this point, "but we haven't gotten that communication to a level where we're actually solving the problems. And that's what AGIA's intended to do, is set up the opportunity, the imperative, the sense of we'd better have that level of communication."

Open season concern

Huggins, who in 2008 would be a leader in opposing approval of an AGIA license for TransCanada, said he shared Palmer's concern that there would be an unsuccessful open season—after which AGIA requires a licensee to proceed through a FERC certificate. He said he hears Palmer saying TransCanada doesn't want to do that "because it's a disaster and what I'm saying and what I hope for is there's phone calls and sitting down in meetings between the key players. It's got to happen," he said. Huggins said his confidence in a successful open season under AGIA was "not very high."

Irwin told the committee that TransCanada framed its issue and he'd like to hear others frame their issues—"what they need and don't need; what they're willing to do and not do. That needs to be framed. Until then, the state is in a very precarious situation, borderline hostage situation" of being told "we need everything—we need fiscal certainty."

The other parties—the producers—have not framed what it will really take, Irwin said.

"And if it takes everything the state has, then I don't think we've all done a correct job, either. We need a framing of their situation: AGIA does that for the state," Irwin said, referring to the "must haves" included in the AGIA bill.

Huggins said his bottom line is that if there is an unsuccessful open season, "Guess who's going to get leveraged? Good old uncle Alaska. In my estimation that's a scary proposition."

Palmer said TransCanada recognized the need for the state to change the dynamics: "We do accept the necessity that the state has put forward AGIA in an attempt to change the dynamics of the project."

TransCanada thinks the key issue in advancing the project is attracting customers, Palmer told the committee.

AGIA is the state's initiative to try to do that; TransCanada has "a difference of opinion with the state" as to whether, after an initial open season which fails to attract enough volume for a successful project, the AGIA licensee should be required to proceed to a FERC certificate. Palmer had pointed out to the committee earlier that the company has held a conditional FERC certificate for the project for 30 years, and he said TransCanada believes "there are other initiatives that can proceed beyond an initial open season, if it does not capture sufficient customers. There are initiatives that we as a commercial party can take, although limited, to see if we can improve the offer, see if we've made a mistake somewhere. And we clearly would have discussions with customers to see if we could improve that situation. I suspect that governments may also wish to do that," he said.

Will producers sell their gas?

Galvin told Senate Resources that in addition to the competition the administration is trying to set up with AGIA, which means not trying to shape requirements or demands around any particular possible AGIA applicant, AGIA is also an attempt to clearly state the question to the producers: "Will you sell your gas at a certain price? Or will you accept a certain tariff rate and agree to commit your gas?"

There is a "tremendous value" for the state in knowing the answer, and with AGIA the administration is trying to create an opportunity for the best project to get to that open season point where that question will be on the table.

If the producers do not commit gas at an open season under AGIA, if they're not willing to commit at that price, then one of the reasons may be "they feel that there isn't sufficient design, sideboards, on the project at that initial open season; that it hasn't been fully fleshed out to where the uncertainty associated with the tariff has been reduced to the point where they're comfortable."

By moving the project through the next phase, through FERC certification, "you will have a different question being placed on them then at the initial open season," the question of willingness to participate in a certificated project.

If there isn't participation in an open season after a FERC certificate is issued, then "something's wrong." Either the project is no longer economic—or never was economic—or there's something the state isn't seeing.

"But in the end what we're all trying to get to, is, we're trying to get to a successful open season. And the question is, if we have that initial open season and we don't get the commitment, is that the point where we say OK we'll try something else?

"We're not ready to say that at this point," Galvin said.

Kern River

Kern River Gas Transmission Co., part of MidAmerican Energy Holdings Co., believes alignment for an Alaska gas pipeline will require the State of Alaska, the North Slope producers, future North Slope explorers and producers, a pipeline developer, shippers and the federal government, Kirk Morgan, Kern River's president, testified before both the House Special Committee on Oil and Gas and the Senate Resources Committee in late March.

MidAmerican, which was interested in the gas pipeline during the Murkowski administration, is a subsidiary of Berkshire Hathaway Inc.

"From our perspective, the negotiations conducted by the previous administration under the stranded gas act were not fruitful for many reasons, foremost among these were that the produced proposals were not supported by the people of the state; they failed to give serious consideration to alternate proposals for development and they consumed years without advancing the project," Kern told House Oil and Gas.

Morgan said Kern River believes AGIA "is a positive step towards revitalizing the gas pipeline development process in a way that will move the project forward."

He said MidAmerican believes there are issues that need to be resolved, but believes "the project can be advanced concurrent with resolutions" of those issues. MidAmerican does believe that "alignment of stakeholder interests is essential."

"Parties will understandably act in their self-interest and in their own business interest. That is why stakeholder alignment is critical to a successful project," he said.

Concern about field season

Asked by Oil and Gas Chair Vic Kohring, R-Wasilla, whether there was anything in AGIA that Kern River would like to see modified to make the bill better, Morgan said Kern River had some concern about the schedule of passing the legislation and getting out the requests for applications, followed by public review, evaluation and selection of an AGIA licensee in time to get into the field in 2008. "Even a month or two of delay ends up costing the project a year in terms of in-service if you miss the field season; that's a significant issue," Morgan said.

AGIA proposed 10 years of contractual tax certainty for those committing gas in an initial open season. Rep. Nancy Dahlstrom, R-Anchorage, asked what Kern River's position was on the 10 years.

Rep. Vic Kohring

Morgan said Kern River believes 10 years is not the life of the project and that the tax rate needs to be negotiated for the life of the project. He suggested that perhaps when resource owners are committing gas, that "perhaps the tax certainty can be structured around that quantity of gas being committed, rather than a period of time."

"That would leave the Legislature open to change its tax regime for new exploration or development drilling going forward, but the resource

Rep. Nancy Dahlstrom

being committed at the time of the open season would have tax certainty," Morgan said.

The open season issue

Dahlstrom also asked about concerns around an unsuccessful open season.

Morgan said he didn't think any company could currently say the project was economic because the last bottoms-up cost estimate was done in 2001 and a lot has changed since then.

He also said he didn't think "the North Slope producers will boycott an open season if the project is economic."

By the time an open season is held, Kern River would expect to have definitive costs and be able to show that the project was or was not economic.

And if the project is economic, "I don't think that the producers have an interest in withholding the gas from an open season." If the project was demonstrated to be economic and the producers withheld their gas, they would be subject to scrutiny from the U.S. Department of Energy, from the Federal Energy Regulatory Commission, from the state, Congress, shareholders and the public.

As for advancing the project beyond an unsuccessful open season, Morgan said Kern River believes it should. Kern River has "six or seven different expansion scenarios on the shelf. We want to be prepared to react immediately when the market signals are there."

Morgan said, "... marketing timing is very important and we believe the project needs to be advanced and should be advanced through a certification by FERC."

House Majority Leader Ralph Samuels, R-Anchorage, asked about continuing after a failed open season and Morgan said: "If it is clear to us that the project is economic and the open season fails because people wouldn't commit their gas because maybe they want to build the pipeline rather than us, we would continue to FERC certification. If the open season fails because the project isn't economic, that's a different matter, and there's a different provision in AGIA dealing with whether the project is economic or not, but we would certainly advance the project if the project appears to be economic to us, we (would) advance it to certification."

Samuels—who in May would be the only member of the Legislature to vote against passage of AGIA—said that after listening to economists talk about the project being economic or not economic (during the previous year's stranded gas hearings), "the frustration we all have is that since those three companies (the North Slope producers) have the gas and we feel we are leveraged by those three companies, at the end of the day all three roads lead to those three companies."

If AGIA is approved and the state partners with MidAmerican, and there is a failed open season, and the reason given "is the same reason that we always hear—that the taxes are too high—now I'm getting leveraged by you and them," Samuels said. "And all roads lead back to them (the producers); leverage doesn't go away because ... instead of Exxon saying well we'll come to the open season if you do this with the taxes ... now it's you saying it. ... I tried to get the gas and I couldn't get it."

It could be in a second Palin term, he said, it could be another governor.

What the state will hear, Samuels said, is "if you just give them this they'll show up at this next open season. And the leverage doesn't go away." He asked Morgan where the leverage goes away.

Instead of being leveraged by ExxonMobil et al, Samuels said I'd have "Warren Buffet (head of Berkshire Hathaway) and Rex Tillerson (CEO of ExxonMobil) leveraging me: It's not pretty; it's not getting any better."

Morgan said tax stability was the issue. "Are the assumptions that I make in my investment today, when I'm making the investment, are they durable? I think that's very valid: To do otherwise is a bait and switch," he said.

The tax level will be factored into the economic analysis of the project, which will be commercial or it won't, Morgan said. "I don't think that you have the information today to say whether you need to reduce taxes or whether this project might be wildly economic and you don't need to do anything."

What's important is once the investment decision is made, that the rules of the game don't change, Morgan said.

The pipeline owner feels the same way, Morgan said, not wanting to hear from FERC 10 years out that the return rate approved for the investment is no longer valid.

He said Kern River (which ultimately did not submit an AGIA application) would be including some long-term investment protection to deal with those issues in its proposal.

Morgan said that prior to open season Kern River would have "a top-to-bottom cost estimate; that will be the cost estimate that is going in a FERC filing." That estimate will give the state the information it needs to know whether it needs to cut taxes. But he said again he did not think that 10 years was long enough; he thought tax stability should be for the volume of gas committed in an initial open season. He said he apologized if he was aligning with the producers, "but that's just how we view the investment."

There are three types of people: those who hoped something would happen; those who watched things happen; and those who made things happen. As far as a gas pipeline goes, the state had "hoped and wished and watched" and "we're at the point where we can make something happen. We can take this issue into the state's hands and we can drive this forward."

—Tom Irwin, commissioner of the Department of Natural Resources

Chapter 8

Palin victory: AGIA debate and passage

Upon passage of AGIA, Rep. Beth Kerttula, D-Juneau, the House minority leader, thanked the governor for her leadership, for "all of your hard work and your willingness to listen to us and to keep your door open right up until late last night. I really appreciate it as do the members of my caucus."

By Kristen Nelson

Gov. Sarah Palin promised Alaskans that her Alaska Gasline Inducement Act would ensure a gas pipeline project, open the North Slope basin to long-term exploration and production, create jobs for Alaskans, and ensure gas for Alaskans. "These bedrock principles protect Alaska's long-term interests, and were, unfortunately, missing from the draft contract proposed by the previous administration," the governor wrote in a mid-February 2007 gas line briefing.

Administration and Legislature shared the goal of getting Alaska North Slope natural gas to market, but, as always, the devil was in the details, and it took collaboration, cooperation and what one legislator described as divine intervention to get AGIA approved by the end of the legislative session in mid-May 2007.

While there was grumbling, and concern among some legislators that AGIA was so prescriptive that the North Slope producers—BP, ConocoPhillips and ExxonMobil—would not apply and would not commit gas to a pipeline they did not build, the popularity of the gas line project and the governor carried the day: Final approval was 20-0 in the Senate; 37-1 in the House, with two members absent.

Introduced in March

AGIA, introduced in early March 2007, required applicants to meet a number of state requirements in exchange for inducements which included $500 million in state matching funds for work leading to a Federal Energy Regulatory Commission certificate for a gas pipeline, a permit coordinator and a training program for the workforce needed for the project.

The ideas that the process needed to be competitive, that it needed to be open and that the state needed to establish what it was willing to do and what it needed—the state's bottom line—were ideas Palin talked about during her campaign, Commissioner of Revenue Pat Galvin said in a September 2008 interview.

Those things came from the governor, from the new administration, he said: They weren't created by the gas line team.

Galvin told House and Senate committees in mid-March 2007 that what the state would get in exchange for the $500 million included the project moving forward, lower tariffs, commitments for pipeline expansions as needed and rolled-in rates, a tariff methodology which averages rates for existing and expansion shippers, encouraging companies without known reserves to explore for gas.

The commitment to go all the way to a FERC certificate—even if an initial open season wasn't successful in attracting sufficient commitments to ship gas—was crucial, Galvin said in 2008. Once the gas line team realized it needed a commitment all the way to a FERC certificate, the question became "How are we ever going to get somebody to agree to do that? What are we going to have to put in (AGIA) to actually get somebody willing to take on that commitment, because that's a big deal; it's a billion-dollar spend." That was when the decision was made that AGIA would include up to $500 million in matching funds, in exchange for the commitment that the applicant would get a FERC certificate.

Making it happen

Department of Natural Resources Commissioner Tom Irwin said AGIA was the state's opportunity to make a gas pipeline happen.

There are three types of people, he told legislators at March 2007 AGIA hearings: those who hope something would happen; those who watched things happen; and those who made things happen.

As far as a gas pipeline goes, the state had "hoped and wished and watched," he said, and "we're at the point where we can make something happen. We can take this issue into the state's hands and we can drive this forward."

Irwin said he'd heard comments about the state "giving away" $500 million as part of AGIA.

That's as far from the truth as possible, he said: There's nothing wrong with anyone who owns assets of great value investing in those assets. "It's appropriate."

Irwin said he expected to hear that we wouldn't need the $500 million as a driver, but said that if that was taken away, then the state would slip back into either watching things happen or hoping things would happen.

"We clearly want to be driving this," he said, calling the $500 million an investment in Alaska's resources that we want to start getting to market.

State's urgency is not necessarily industry's

Moving the project forward was worth money, Galvin told legislators during AGIA testimony in March 2007, because it costs the state revenues for every year the gas line project slipped. Lower tariffs also drove value to the state because the state collects taxes on the net value at the wellhead, which was lower the higher the tariff was, and the state paid the tariff on its own royalty gas.

"There is a bit of a disconnect in alignment between the urgency felt by the State of Alaska in terms of developing natural gas resources and that felt by ... the energy industry as a whole," Kurt Gibson, acting deputy director of the division of oil and gas, told legislators. He said the administration wanted to change behaviors and was willing to put up money to do that.

If the price for natural gas was $5.50 in Chicago, "the state recoups three times the capital contribution," some $1.8 billion, "simply by accelerating the project by a single year." If the March 2007 price of $6.75 in Chicago held, the state would recover five times the capital contribution by accelerating the project a single year, he told legislators.

The bill required a licensee to complete an open season within three years of award of the license and allowed another 24 months for FERC certification, assuming pre-filing activity at FERC by the AGIA licensee, Gibson said.

Tariff reduction

The state's contribution would be in the form of a grant, and would not be paid back, so it would reduce the pipeline tariff by 4 cents to 6 cents for 30 years, Gibson said, and in real financial terms "for every penny change in the tariff, the state realizes $45 million in royalty and production tax" over the life of the project. For 4 cents, that would be $180 million; for 6 cents it would be $270 million.

That $500 million would buy the state a list of "must haves," what any project proponent must do, "but in addition you're getting something back by locking in certain debt-equity ratio percentages." And because the $500 million was a capital contribution to the project— not an equity position—the economics of basin development would be improved for everyone, Gibson said.

Antony Scott, acting chief of the division of oil and gas commercial section, told legislators the bill's requirement of 70 percent debt and 30 percent equity ensured a lower tariff and increased the present value of state revenue from the project by some $2.5 billion, compared to tariff rates based on 50 percent debt and 50 percent equity.

House Majority Leader Ralph Samuels, R-Anchorage, asked about the ability of companies to get financing at the proposed 70-30 ratio, and Scott said 70-30 was what an AGIA licensee would be required to submit to FERC for rate-base building, and would not necessarily be the same as the actual debt-equity ratio in the financing.

Expansion required

AGIA required an expansion provision for the pipeline. Without it, said Kevin Banks, acting director of the state division of oil and gas, "I think that the exploration for new gas in the North Slope will be hampered considerably."

With the three-year timeline, only a few explorers would be able to commit gas in an initial open season. The federal government has estimated some 200 trillion cubic feet of technically recoverable undiscovered gas onshore and offshore the North Slope. While those volumes aren't necessarily economically recoverable, Banks said, the requirement in AGIA for the pipeline to hold regular open seasons and expand when economic volumes of new gas are nominated allows explorers "a regular opportunity" to nominate gas and would make more discoveries economic because of a known timeframe.

A thumbs up from Gov. Sarah Palin, who went to Fairbanks on June 6, 2007, for a ceremonial signing of her gas pipeline legislation, the Alaska Gasline Inducement Act. Pictured from left to right: Bonnie Harris, Bruce Anders, Antony Scott, Sarah Palin, Virgie King, Kurt Gibson and Sean Parnell.

Rolled-in rates are required for expansion as long as the increase was not more than 15 percent, Scott said, which also would make prospects that are already economic, more profitable.

Rep. Carl Gatto, R-Palmer, asked whether that would make all existing shippers opposed to expansions.

"Initial shippers, if they have an interest in expansion themselves, in general will favor rolled-in rate treatment for expansion costs," Scott said, "assuming that they don't also own the pipeline," because rolled-in rates make exploration prospects more economic.

Galvin added that the short answer to the question was "yes."

"If you are an initial shipper and you don't have any more gas that you intend to ever ship other than the steady stream of your initial, then you would oppose rolled-in rates simply because you would see an increase because ... basically there's more demand for what you're taking advantage of than what there was before," Galvin said.

Other oil and gas views

Oil and gas companies other than BP, ConocoPhillips and ExxonMobil had different views on AGIA than the producers.

Chevron's new ventures manager, Vince LeMieux, told legislators that an Alaska natural gas pipeline project would be so big it would create its own weather, driving behaviors in steel and labor markets. He said he worried that if Chevron was successful in its current North Slope exploration efforts at its White Hills prospect, he would have to get those facilities in before the pipeline came along because it would take precedence, soaking up resources and putting other projects on hold. (White Hills is primarily an oil prospect, but it also a gas-prone area.)

David Keane, vice president of policy and corporate affairs for BG America, an international natural gas company, said the line would be a mega project requiring tremendous efforts on a number of fronts. He said the $500 million in matching funds in AGIA was an inducement to get serious pipeline companies involved because it demonstrated to industry that Alaska was serious about moving the project forward.

The project cost will be critical, as will fiscal issues, LeMieux said. There are huge uncertainties about how the tariff would work, and that, he said, was what determined how the rent from the project was shared up and down the value chain.

Access to the line for explorers—those without gas to commit at an initial open season—was another area where risk was shared and where there was an opportunity for misalignment, he said.

LeMieux said the bill was a "great step forward," that it created a mechanism to engage people in discussion on how to frame the project. But the bill could change the fundamental economics, and

LeMieux said he always returned to asking himself whether he understood how the project would work and make money for participants up and down the line.

The water trough was full and he was not quite sure what you could do to lead the horses to water, BG's Keane said, but told legislators he thought AGIA was the right vehicle to get the ball rolling and start discussions.

BG wouldn't have gas to commit initially, and so was concerned about access and expansion; more certainty of access was a benefit of having the line built by an independent pipeline company, he said in response to a question from Sen. Tom Wagoner, R-Kenai.

Keane noted that an independent pipeline company increased its revenue by increasing its throughput, so having a company like BG find gas on the North Slope was a benefit to an independent line.

Keane noted BG was also a producer, and said it might not be in his best interest as a producer to allow other companies to come into a line it owned. The short version, he said, was that he'd rather have a pipeline owner with the incentive to increase revenues by increasing throughput, rather than a pipeline owner/gas producer who could increase his revenue by decreasing other producers' throughput.

Anadarko looking for gas

Anadarko Petroleum would like to be able to commit gas in an initial open season for an Alaska natural gas pipeline under AGIA, but was unlikely to be able to discover and prove up gas if that open season occurred in the next three to three and a half years, Mark Hanley, the company's public affairs manager for Alaska, told Senate Resources in March 2007.

Anadarko needed to do enough gas drilling to hold its leases, without putting too much money into exploring if a gas pipeline didn't go ahead in the next few years, he said.

With four prospects in the North Slope Foothills, Anadarko contracted for a new rig and planned to drill in the winter of 2007-08. (While no results were available from that exploration drilling,

Anadarko and partners did drill and test one well and drilled almost half of a second, with plans to double its exploration effort in the winter of 2008-09 and get three wells drilled, which would include finishing the partly drilled well.)

Pipeline shippers take long-term risks, "and we can't make a long-term commitment without understanding the field and how it's going to perform," Hanley told legislators. Once it knew it had enough gas, Anadarko would ask for an expansion in the line—likely achievable with additional compression, a decision the gas line owner would have to make.

FORREST CRANE

Mark Hanley, Anadarko

Hanley said Anadarko was concerned about a producer-owned pipeline because it believed motivations change a bit "when you have a producer-owned pipe versus an independent pipe."

A natural tension—the pipeline owner arguing for a higher rate of return and shippers arguing for a lower rate—wasn't necessarily there with a producer-owned pipeline, he said.

A higher rate of return meant a higher tariff and a lower wellhead value for shippers, both explorers and producers. "But if you're aligned as a producer and a pipeline owner ... it's kind of (from) one pocket into another."

And the state would also be affected, he said, because "the higher the tariff is the lower the state's share because of the wellhead value (price less transportation cost)."

While supporting AGIA, Hanley said Anadarko disagreed with fiscal certainty for only those committing gas in an initial open season—when Anadarko likely wouldn't have gas to commit. You could come in two years later—after the initial open season but long before the line was completed—and your gas would still be some of the first shipped down the line, but you wouldn't have fiscal certainty, he said.

Big 3 producers objected

The North Slope producers, as expected, objected to AGIA.

While they believed a North Slope gas pipeline was essential for Alaska's future—and to meet natural gas needs in the Lower 48 states—the producers told legislators they did not think AGIA was the way to get that line built.

Martin "Marty" Massey, ExxonMobil's U.S. joint interest manager, said the State of Alaska needed to provide fiscal certainty (commit to levels for taxes and royalties) for longer than the 10 years provided in AGIA. He said each applicant under AGIA should describe what fiscal terms were necessary and the state should evaluate that as part of the applications.

Galvin said the ExxonMobil message "is consistent." This is what the company has been telling the state for a number of years—fiscal certainty not just on gas production taxes but on oil production tax, property tax, corporate income tax and royalties. "Clearly that is their stated position," Galvin told legislators.

He said the changes ExxonMobil proposed to AGIA were on the model of the Stranded Gas Development Act, which Galvin said was a model Exxon was comfortable with. Under that model applicants would respond to broad requirements and the administration would probably have to negotiate and bring those results back to the Legislature. Exxon is successful in leverage in negotiations, Galvin said, positioning itself so its position has the greatest strength.

The state could do what it did under the stranded gas act and try to negotiate with the producers, he said, or it could try something new as proposed in AGIA where the state set out—in advance—its requirements in exchange for stated incentives.

BP, Conoco also objected

Dave Van Tuyl, gas commercialization manager for BP in Alaska, told legislators BP believed AGIA "may create some unintended consequences that could jeopardize the vision of getting Alaska's gas to market quickly and at low cost."

BP was concerned that AGIA "would result in an exclusive winner before any real work is done," awarding state funds based on promises, not on results, he said.

Van Tuyl suggested the state ask project sponsors to propose mid-stream incentives, rather than specifying them in advance, giving "the free market the opportunity to do what it does best. The state could then determine what inducements to offer and perhaps make those available to all parties to allow competition."

Like ExxonMobil, BP said AGIA "doesn't sufficiently address the resource framework." Resource owners would pay the cost and would bear the risk of the pipeline, whether they owned it or not, Van Tuyl said. Resource issues had to be resolved in order for the project to move forward, he said, ensuring that resource owners would have the confidence to make long-term financial commitments required in an open season.

ConocoPhillips agreed with the state that timing would be important for an Alaska gas pipeline project, but was concerned about the exclusive nature of AGIA in selecting a single project.

Wendy King, director of state negotiations for ConocoPhillips, asked why the state would want to block competing projects with inducements provided only to the selected project. If the state chose the wrong winner and that project didn't go forward, other projects could be blocked for 10 years, she said.

She said the company was eager to find a framework by which both the midstream and the resource parts of the project could be advanced.

No surprise

Palin, speaking at a press conference at the end of March 2007, said it was no surprise to her that the producers and those wishing to do business with them would acknowledge "how good they had it, I guess, under the Murkowski administration, in terms of what was being given to them in order to induce them to perhaps—someday—build a gas line."

She described AGIA as "a fair and transparent process where we're not going to be giving away the farm in order to induce or entice three big producers to come to the State of Alaska and help develop our gas resources."

Palin said Alaska had "good support" for AGIA on the national level, relating that she had updated Vice President Dick Cheney on progress just that week. "He continued to express his support for getting a gas line built, knowing that it is in the nation's best interest," she said.

Palin said she was "very committed to AGIA and convinced this is the right road to go down."

She said she wanted Alaskans to be able to benefit from the state's gas resources with gas for in-state use and with jobs.

Bill changed

The Legislature did a lot of work on AGIA, which was introduced as House Bill 177, the bill eventually passed by the Legislature, and as Senate Bill 104. Those bills passed their respective bodies May 11, 2007—the Senate bill unanimously, the House bill (with only 38 representatives voting), 37 in favor and House Majority Leader Ralph Samuels opposed.

Committees in both bodies did a lot of work on AGIA, making both technical and substantive changes.

One change they made was in the approval process for an AGIA license.

The administration had proposed that once the administration completed the public comment process and the commissioners of Natural Resources and Revenue issued a decision recommending that a license be issued, the Legislature would have 30 days to reject that recommendation, otherwise the license would automatically be issued. The administration said that would provide a safety valve on the process and the Legislature wouldn't even have to meet if there was general agreement with the administration's recommendation.

Legislators wanted to do their own evaluation of a proposed AGIA license and changed the provision to require legislative approval before a license could be issued. The Legislature gave itself 60 days from the

time the president of the Senate and the speaker of the House officially received the license recommendation to vote that approval.

If the Legislature failed to approve the license, it would fail.

Another substantive change was in how the applications would be
evaluated. The original bill included a list of things the commissioners
would consider in evaluating the applications, but legislators wanted a
system for comparing and ranking competing proposals.

The final bill provided that applications which met all of the state's
requirements—20 so-called "must haves"—would be evaluated based
on the net present value of the anticipated cash flow to the state
weighted by the likelihood of the project's success based on six factors
listed in AGIA.

Effort to parallel

The administration worked to keep the two versions of the bill as
similar as possible in order to avoid a conference committee at the end
of the session faced with resolving differences. In
2006 it took three tries—in the regular session and
in two special sessions—before conference committees could resolve differences between versions of the
big oil and gas bill in that Legislature, the petroleum
profits/production tax.

House Speaker John Harris, R-Valdez, said at the
end of April that legislators were trying to avoid a
conference committee to reconcile House and Senate

Rep. John Harris

versions of AGIA because of concern that would drive the Legislature
into a special session. There were three special sessions in the summer
of 2006 and legislators did not seem anxious to spend another summer in Juneau.

As a result, the bills that passed May 11 were very similar.

A Senate Finance substitute for the House bill dealt with differences and both bodies approved the Senate substitute for HB 177, the
Senate the day before the session ended and the House about 10:40
p.m. on the final day of the session.

Sen. Bert Stedman, R-Sitka, co-chair of Senate Finance, said on the Senate floor that most of the issues where the House version was chosen involved wordsmithing. On more substantive issues, he said, the Senate version was selected, including expanding qualified expenditures of the $500 million state matching funds to include "pursuing firm transportation commitments in a binding open season, to secure financing for the project." The House version said the money could be used to obtain a FERC or Regulatory Commission of Alaska certificate for the gas line. Stedman said the change would allow an AGIA licensee that didn't obtain sufficient firm transportation commitments at an initial binding open season to spend more time trying to hold a successful open season while pursuing a certificate. Another Senate change excluded lobbying costs from qualified expenditures which the state would match.

House Finance Co-Chair Mike Chenault, R-Nikiski, said on the House floor May 16 that the final bill contained 16 items from the House version and six from the Senate, including making all applications—incomplete as well as complete—available to the public. Chenault said that was in the interest of "transparency and openness and fairness to all applicants."

"I think that we've done our job," he said. "I think we've put together a package that hopefully allows the governor and her people to go out and get a pipeline project." The Senate vote was 20 to zero; the House vote was 37 to 1.

AGIA passes

When AGIA passed—separate versions in the House and Senate on May 11 and final passage May 15 in the Senate and May 16 in the House—the administration had its vehicle for moving forward.

"This is a great day for Alaska," the governor said May 11 after the separate bills passed in the House and Senate.

But there's many a slip between cup and lip, and even though there was basic agreement May 11, the route to final House approval May 16 was dicey—and apparently negotiated partly with help from the FBI.

The FBI searched offices of six Alaska legislators in August 2006.

On May 3, 2007, three indictments were issued and on May 4, one sitting legislator and two former legislators were arrested, charged with accepting bribes to influence the vote on the 2006 petroleum profits/production tax.

Palin commented May 11 that there was "a world of difference" from the previous Friday—the day of the FBI arrests.

"I have a lot of hope for Alaska after the actions of our lawmakers today being able to provide that hope," she said. The state was now "going to go forward with a process of trying to get a gas line built for Alaska, for our future, that's going to be built on trust and transparency, openness. That's what AGIA is all about, so there's a world of difference between today and a week ago."

Legislature also pleased

Legislators also commented after the May 11 passage of the House and Senate versions of AGIA.

Sen. Bert Stedman, R-Ketchikan, co-chair of Senate Finance and a member of the Senate majority, thanked the governor for "all her hard work and her willingness to work in a very open and transparent way with the entire Legislature" in moving AGIA. He said the majority in the Senate (the Senate Bipartisan Working Group), the House and the Senate minority all worked together. Both the House and the Senate worked with the administration "to move the state forward and work the best AGIA bill in concept that the Legislature and the administration could put together."

This was only one step on the road to a gas pipeline, he said, but it was still historic.

Stedman said Alaska's Permanent Fund would likely be sitting at around $90 billion by the time gas flowed.

"If we have problems along the way, the state is going to step up and further push for the construction of this gas line and we'll have the financial clout and ability to muscle it forward if that's what it takes to get it built," Stedman said.

Sen. Hollis French, D-Anchorage, also a member of the Senate majority, said he hoped "today's the day we're driving the golden spike, the first spike" in a line to take Alaska's North Slope gas to market.

Sen. Gene Therriault, R-North Pole, the Senate minority leader, said that while the Senate minority had been onboard with the governor from the beginning, they continued to question and had Commissioner Galvin come by that morning to explain the most recent changes in the bill.

A consultant hired by the Legislature also heard the explanations and Therriault said that after Galvin left he asked the consultant his view: Would the bill as crafted move the project forward?

The consultant said it probably wasn't perfect, but that he believed AGIA would start the ball rolling in the right direction.

Therriault said this consultant was a former oil and gas executive, so he asked what the buzz was nationwide about what Alaska was doing.

Sen. Gene Therriault

"And the indication was that the buzz is very positive, that the feeling is that the State of Alaska is looking out for its own best interests, but also doing so in a way that really gets the momentum going on this project," Therriault said.

Rep. Beth Kerttula, D-Juneau, the House minority leader, thanked the governor for her leadership, for "all of your hard work and your willingness to listen to us and to keep your door open right up until late last night. I really appreciate it as do the members of my caucus," she said.

Rep. Mike Chenault, R-Nikiski, co-chair of House Finance, thanked the governor and the commissioners for all the hard work that had gone into the project.

"I think it is a good day in Alaska; hopefully, we move forward," he said.

The next hurdle would be the applications, Chenault said. He said he hoped there would be more than one proposal, and said while he'd like to see five or six, "if we have more than one, I think maybe this is a success."

Chenault did say that there were still concerns that AGIA wasn't open enough to allow all entities to participate. There were discussions about changes, he said. "I don't believe the votes were there to make any major changes to this bill ... but I think that what we have before us today is our best chance at moving forward on a gas line right now."

Rep. Beth Kerttula

Rep. Carl Gatto, R-Palmer, co-chair of House Resources, credited passage of AGIA to cooperation.

"You know the reason we're here in 2007 and not 2008 or 2009 or 2010 is because the House worked with the Senate; the Senate worked with the House; the Democrats worked with the Republicans; the Republicans worked with the Democrats; and the whole bunch of us worked with the administration and the governor and that's why it's 2007 and not some other time."

But the thing I'll remember, Gatto said, is that when AGIA showed up in Resources it was 20 pages long (it was more than 30 pages when passed) and the committee took up 57 amendments—all but one, of which, he said, passed.

Exit strategy

Palin said at a May 17 press conference, the day after the Legislature adjourned, that before the FBI arrests the administration was being asked what its exit strategy was.

"Talk about down to the wire. I think last night could be characterized as a nail biter," she said, referring to the House's final passage of the Senate Finance Committee substitute for AGIA just before 11 p.m. May 16—the session ended at midnight.

Palin related that the day before that last day there was a chasm "the size of Hurricane Gulch (site of a 918-foot railroad crossing some 300 feet above the Chulitna River in the Matanuska-Susitna Borough), between proposals and between personalities."

She said one lawmaker had told her "that unless there was some kind of divine intervention, that there was no way things were going to come together and we're going to have to go into overtime."

One good proposal

Palin called AGIA the vehicle that would get Alaska a gas line.

"It's fair; it's inviting to all; it lets the marketplace do what it does best. Through competition it allows the best project and the best partners to be chosen for Alaska to get us a gas line," the governor said after final passage.

She said she would like to see multiple proposals, but "in order to get a pipeline built, we need one good proposal. We need the right proposal."

Deputy DNR Commissioner Marty Rutherford, head of the governor's gas line team, agreed that what the state needed was one good proposal, but said applications could come from consortiums, "so we're hoping that we have multiple parties interested in competing."

The project is a lucrative one, she said, "and we're comfortable that we're going to get multiple applications."

The next step was a request for applications and the administration said it hoped to have a licensee selected and approved by the Legislature so that field work for a gas pipeline could begin in the summer of 2008.

Palin said RFA language was already being crafted.

The goal was to have the RFA out by the first of July.

Reprinted from the Aug. 12, 2007 Petroleum News. The news of the arrests and ongoing corruption investigation of Alaska politicians would have a number of impacts, including the loss of one strong bidder for a license under the Alaska Gasline Inducement Act.

Bank on MidAmerican

Pipeline giant to file Alaska gas line application, despite pressure to drop out

By Kay Cashman
Petroleum News

MidAmerican Energy and its partners plan to submit an application to the State of Alaska to build a natural gas pipeline from the North Slope, David L. Sokol told Petroleum News Aug. 7. Sokol is CEO of MidAmerican Energy Holdings Co., parent of Kern River Gas Transmission Co., which has served as MidAmerican's lead for the Alaska gas line project.

A GLANCE FORWARD

David L. Sokol

The only thing that could stand in the way of MidAmerican's application, he said, was if the FBI investigations and indictments of Alaska State and U.S. lawmakers would somehow "circle back to implicate any of the producers. If they do, our concern is the process might negatively impact a gas line project from a timing standpoint."

Applications for a project to take North Slope gas to Lower 48 markets have to be filed under the Alaska Gasline Inducement Act by Nov. 30. Strongly supported by Alaska Gov. Sarah Palin, AGIA passed at the end of the 2007 legislative session despite intense criticism from the North Slope's three oil producers and gas owners, BP, ConocoPhillips and ExxonMobil. The three mega-majors, which own controlling inter-

est in the 800-mile trans-Alaska oil pipeline, have indicated it's imperative they also own controlling interest in a gas line in order to keep project costs down. They say AGIA, as written, won't work.

The three companies have not said whether they will file a pipeline
application. Paul Laird, general manager of the Alaska Support Industry
Alliance, told Petroleum News Aug. 8 that he expects two of the three
companies to file, "possibly with partners, one or more applications that
do not conform to AGIA's specifications."

Sokol's openness unusual

The fact that Sokol would say whether or not MidAmerican was
preparing an application was unusual, but he believed the circumstances
warranted it.

"We wouldn't normally answer that question because it is a competitive situation, but I would say it has been startling to us how many people and organizations have been trying to infiltrate our team to find out
the answer to that question. There have been quite a number of people
trying to dissuade us from applying, or do things of that nature," he
said.

Calls rumors about Morgan 'malicious'

Another irritant for the pipeline giant has been the rumor that Kern
River President Kirk Morgan was fired by MidAmerican at the end of
May because of his positive testimony on AGIA to the Alaska
Legislature—a rumor that Sokol called "malicious" and "inappropriate."

Sokol said he and Morgan were "on the same page" regarding the
Alaska gas line project and that Morgan "was not fired. Not by any
means. Frankly, we considered Kirk one of our most valuable senior
managers. He made a decision for personal, family reasons to take an
early retirement. We preferred that he stayed, but we respected his decision. We would welcome him back tomorrow."

The rumor about Morgan "is just another effort by some of the
folks who don't want the pipeline built … under AGIA, and wish to
discredit efforts under AGIA. It's insulting people would even make

such accusations," Sokol said.

"We will continue to work on the pipeline application," he said. "Our intention is to file under AGIA, but whether we do depends on the circumstances between now and the filing date. The unfortunate corruption scandals involving the oil and gas industry in Alaska that have been published in the press ... we just don't know where it will stop. ... It's very good Alaska's had a change in administrations and we support the Palin administration. But you have two members of the Alaska Congressional delegation under investigation, allegations made against another, and indictments against state legislators. We know only what we read in the news. We don't know where those indictments will stop."

MidAmerican will apply with partners

When asked if MidAmerican and Kern River would submit a gas line application with partners, Sokol said yes, but he would not reveal the identity of those partners because he was concerned they would be subjected to the same pressure MidAmerican has been.

"In light of the pressure that's been put on us, we think we are doing our potential partners a favor by not identifying them," he said, noting MidAmerican would name its partners when it was necessary to do so under the AGIA process.

Another rumor

Another rumor circulating in Alaska's oil patch is that the state isn't going to receive any credible bids under AGIA. A version of that rumor has already made its way across the border. Calgary-based Enbridge CEO Pat Daniel told analysts Aug. 1 that his information indicates there is "not a lot of active interest for trying to mount a project without producers' support."

Daniel said Enbridge officials "continue to advise the governor and the state that unless they can get a consortium of producers together to file under the AGIA we won't be a participant in the process."

In his testimony to the Alaska Legislature about AGIA, Morgan said, "even if a pipeline is developed by an independent developer, the North Slope producers will play a critical role as shippers on the line and sellers of gas to other shippers."

"MidAmerican, as an independent pipeline, is impartial and in a unique position to help facilitate solutions where stakeholders' interests diverge," he said, noting that unlike the three producers, MidAmerican had no competing interests in the upstream, downstream or globally.

Morgan also admitted the project was more risky with unwilling gas sellers, but he said, AGIA had mitigated much of that concern—and he believed that if money could be made by selling gas, BP, ConocoPhillips and ExxonMobil shareholders would want the gas sold.

Why is the gas that is owned by the three majors so important to a gas line project?

Despite the fact that government estimates put northern Alaska's undiscovered, technically recoverable natural gas at more than 200 trillion cubic feet, explorers on gas-prone acreage, such as Anadarko and BG, have been reluctant to move forward with exploration and development until they were relatively certain a gas pipeline would be built to take North Slope gas to market.

Hence, expectations that the Prudhoe Bay oil field with its 24.5 trillion cubic feet of discovered gas reserves, would produce the first gas for a pipeline. Prudhoe is essentially owned in equal parts by BP, ConocoPhillips and ExxonMobil, with the fourth largest owner being Chevron, which holds a 1 percent interest.

What about costs?

So, what about costs? Gas prices are high now, but what if they drop? Opponents of an independent gas line say the producers will be more concerned about keeping construction costs low because they'll be shipping gas in the line, whereas a pipeline company such as MidAmerican isn't going be as worried about cost overruns because it can simply charge a tariff based on whatever the pipeline costs them to build.

Petroleum News turned to Alaska Revenue Commissioner Pat

Galvin for an answer.

"You have to look at where a pipeline company makes its money," he said. "They make their money based on how much gas is run through the line. The more gas, the more money for them. If you have a bloated tariff, you're not going to get companies to invest in exploration and development of gas fields on the North Slope to put gas into the line."

Selling gas into the pipeline "has to be economic for gas producers in order for a pipeline company to make a profit." Galvin said. "It's in a pipeline company's best interest to keep the cost of building the line low, so their tariff makes producing gas in Alaska competitive with projects worldwide."

Plus, he said, there are parts of AGIA that deal with cost overruns, making the pipeline company "take some of that risk themselves. It couldn't simply pass along overruns to the gas producers. That's pretty standard elsewhere, in modern pipeline contracts. … That's why we moved this project under AGIA into a transparent process, as compared to the process under the Murkowski administration. Under AGIA we can talk about the level of risk companies take on rather than just speculate."

Galvin also said he's not surprised at the number of rumors in circulation.

"There is a campaign of misinformation going on to give the impression the project under AGIA is dead in the water," he told Petroleum News Aug. 7.

A week earlier, he'd said, "AGIA is a competitive process, so we can expect, and in fact we are seeing, a lot of misdirection and misinformation floated around. … We probably won't know until the application deadline what the parties' true intentions may be."

"I thought the oil fairy would save us again in '09 but what we are finding is that it isn't. … We are going to find we are in a deficit situation."

—Sen. Gary Wilken, R-Fairbanks, April 19, 2007

Chapter 9

Palin raises oil production tax

"I thought the oil fairy would save us again in '09 but what we are finding is that it isn't. … We are going to find we are in a deficit situation."

–Sen. Gary Wilken, R-Fairbanks

By Kay Cashman

This book's jacket promises an account of Palin's "concrete successes and failures in dealing" with Alaska's oil industry.

The three North Slope producers would say that Sarah Palin has failed to communicate with them. They have complained that the governor and her people won't engage in long discussions with them.

The governor, Commissioners Pat Galvin and Tom Irwin, and deputy commissioner Marty Rutherford, have all said that's because the companies wanted to tell them what they have already heard—that fiscal negotiations needed to start where they left off with the Murkowski administration.

Likewise, some of the concessions and benefits for the state and people of Alaska that the Palin administration wrote into the Alaska Gasline Inducement Act, or AGIA, would be considered failures by the three North Slope producers and want-to-be-pipeline owners, BP, ConocoPhillips and ExxonMobil, but from the perspective of the people of Alaska and the oil and gas companies that would not own a piece of the gas line, AGIA was a success.

There was one thing that many Alaskans might have wanted from the governor if they had given it much thought and that was her vocal support for exploration drilling in the Beaufort and Chukchi seas by leaseholders Shell, Repsol, Eni, StatoilHydro, Total and ConocoPhillips—starting two years before when the first of the group, Shell, started planning a Beaufort Sea drilling program.

Since the leases expected to produce the most oil and gas were in federal waters, there wouldn't have been royalties or production taxes

Working with Palin: Pat Galvin

Pat Gavin, commissioner of the Department of Revenue: "For us she's been very positive. ... She's what you'd always want in a CEO in the sense that she provides clear direction in terms of the policy direction that she's trying to accomplish. And she participates in the discussions as a member of the team, she doesn't ... waltz into the room (and) lord over the discussion. ... She'll sit in and engage and listen and take in information and ask questions, and then make an assessment of the situation," a decision.

for the state, but the oil would have helped keep the trans-Alaska oil pipeline full.

Plus, offshore exploration and development would have meant jobs for Alaskans, and work for Alaska oilfield service contractors that pay corporate income tax to the State of Alaska.

Shell program on hold

But Shell's program for exploration drilling in the Beaufort Sea offshore of Alaska's North Slope remained on hold until the U.S. Court of Appeals for the 9th Circuit ruled on an appeal by the North Slope Borough, the Alaska Eskimo Whaling Commission and several environmental organizations against the U.S. Minerals Management Service approval of Shell's exploration plan.

On Aug. 14, 2007, the court placed a temporary injunction on Shell's planned Beaufort Sea drilling, pending a decision in the appeal case. And on Dec. 4, 2007 the court heard oral arguments in the case.

With no ruling from the court as of Oct. 4, 2008, Shell had been unable to drill at its Sivulliq prospect in the Beaufort Sea off Alaska's North Slope.

In June 2008, the company finally cancelled its plans for drilling that summer.

Although Shell has not uttered a word against Palin, the company is disappointed that the court has not yet issued its decision, Pete

Working with Palin: Dan Seamount

Dan Seamount, one of two commissioners who served with Sarah Palin in 2003 and early 2004 on the Alaska Oil and Gas Conservation Commission had the following to say about Palin.

"She's pro-development, not pro-industry. She'll tell you, 'My boss is the people of Alaska.'

"She's smart, a quick study. Her adversaries biggest mistake is underestimating her intelligence, her understanding of issues. And she uses their arrogance against them."

For information on what happened between commissioners Sarah Palin and Randy Ruedrich at

Dan Saemount

AOGCC, read "Palin explains her actions in Ruedrich case," written by Richard Mauer, Anchorage Daily News, Sept. 19, 2004, and available online at http://dwb.adn.com/front/story/5572779p-5504444c.html

Slaiby, Shell's Alaska general manager, told Petroleum News senior staff writer Alan Bailey on Sept. 23.

"Each delay we've got means a delay on first oil and that impacts consumers," Slaiby said in an article Bailey wrote for the Oct. 5 issue of Petroleum News. "… A season clicks by. The first time we'll be able to put a bit in the ground, assuming we get favorable approval, will be 2009."

Shell has other opportunities

As the delays continued Shell needed to consider its other investment opportunities, Slaiby said.

"Shell as a whole has got many, many other places where it can invest," Slaiby said. "... We've just had a major acquisition in Canada."

"I really think this is an opportunity for the State of Alaska and the people of Alaska to get Shell in here," Slaiby said. "Shell's experience in the Arctic and Shell's commitment to local business development and the development of these resources in a responsible and safe, ecologically sound manner is huge."

Working with Palin: Tom Irwin

Tom Irwin, commissioner of the Department of Natural Resources had this to say about Gov. Sarah Palin in a September 2008 interview with Petroleum News:

"I am a conservative Republican. I sometimes wonder where my party has gone, but my governor, Sarah Palin, is bringing it back," he said.

"She's a real leader. You can disagree and she ain't king; she's a leader. ... And you can disagree and argue and we have some hellacious arguments; but never shouting, never ... to the point you're being disrespectful.

"And when she has to make an unpopular decision that might reflect poorly on herself, she says, "I don't care if I take a political hit. We're going to do what's right for Alaska. ...

"What you're allowed to do with this type of leadership is ... it allows you a process where a multitude of heads can get the right answer. ... Now don't misunderstand. This is not management by committee. ... She allowed us to feel we worked with her; but make no doubt about it, she understood it and she was the decision maker. ... It's a management style that's rarely found but hugely successful. ...

"I think a really good manager has to be grounded in fundamentals. ... Our governor ... is grounded in a fundamental of honesty, integrity, her faith and an understanding of the Constitution. ... I've never seen her once, ever, come close to the bright line of wanting to violate those."

Had he received personal criticism from the oil industry?

"When we put the Point Thomson unit in default I got an email that said, 'Go to hell but please resign first,'" Irwin said with a chuckle. He kept that one.

What could Palin, as governor of Alaska, have done to help Shell?

The 9th Circuit was sensitive to the wishes of the local people as demonstrated by its delay in getting out a decision that was sure to be costing Shell hundreds of millions of dollars because of the appeal filed by northern Alaska's North Slope Borough, the Alaska Eskimo Whaling Commission and the Alaska Wilderness League.

A personal plea from the governor to the 9th Circuit and her request that other Alaskans and local development groups get more involved might at least have prompted the court to make a decision.

Production tax gets overhaul

Palin had expressed concern about the new Petroleum Production Tax, or PPT, while she was running for governor, saying she preferred a tax on the gross versus the net.

During her state of the state address in January 2007, she said her administration would carefully watch PPT, noting the structure was untested.

When anticipated PPT revenues fell short of their mark in April 2007, the governor directed Galvin and the Department of Revenue to review the new production tax.

"Within the month, the indictments came out," Galvin told Petroleum News in September 2008. "And so before the legislative session ended, the governor said that the cloud created by the indictments undermined public confidence in the oil tax system and required that it be revisited by the Legislature, and that she intended to call them back in the fall."

In early August 2007 the governor called a special session of the Legislature for Oct. 18, asking legislative leaders to hold it on the road system rather than at the capitol in Juneau (accessible only by air or water), saying that would allow more Alaskans to participate and to "keep an eye on things." (That request went over like a lead balloon. The session was held in Juneau.)

At issue was whether PPT was "delivering on its promise to the Legislature and the public." Another issue was whether PPT was "creating an environment conducive to investment and new exploration needed for a successful future."

Palin said "exploration companies are getting less value from the credits included in PPT than was expected."

There were also "significant" challenges in administering the PPT, she said, "including greater difficulty in forecasting state revenues, the auditing challenges that are being faced and difficulty describing allowable expenditures in the new regulations."

Palin said she had directed Revenue "to prepare a proposal to respond to these deficiencies with PPT—particularly how can we make this fair with our industry partners, how Alaskans can receive appropriate value for these nonrenewable resources so ... we can become less dependent upon the federal government in paying our bills" and also encourage "new investment in exploration and development."

Up to $25 million in credits could be refunded by the state; legislators presumed the companies with credits beyond that would sell them to existing Alaska producers, the report said. "In the first year that the PPT has been in place, however, companies holding credit certificates report that there have been few buyers for the certificates, and that those offering to buy them are doing so at large discounts."

Galvin said Revenue also faced significant challenges in implementing PPT, noting the auditing required was more complex than expected and it had been difficult for the state to attract auditor expertise at state pay levels.

Revenue expected to have a clear proposal ready for legislators in early September, Galvin said. A bill reflecting proposed changes would be ready by Oct. 18, 2007, when the special session began.

Change from gross to hybrid version of net and gross

To develop the new tax system Revenue put together a team that included Revenue economists and accountants, DNR's division of oil and gas commercial analysts, geologists and engineers, outside experts, and attorneys from the private sector and the Department of Law.

"So at that point we were studying both gross-based tax and net-based tax options. Our expectation, mine included, was that we would be able to develop a system based upon gross value with capital credits and some appropriate adjustments for new fields and so forth, but we would have a gross-based tax that could work across the board on the North Slope," Galvin said.

Working with Palin: Marty Rutherford

Marty Rutherford, deputy commissioner of the Department of Natural Resources: "She is directed by facts. She campaigned on a gross tax, but at some point we determined that the best way to go was a net tax, a tax on the profits. We had to drag her kicking and screaming to that conclusion. But she let the facts guide her. ....

"I enjoy working with her. She sets the vision and then lets you do the work. She's responsive to arguments, to debate. ...

"I'm pretty cynical. I've worked with several governors. ... This is the first time I can say I am really quite fond of this governor. ...

"So many governors make decisions on, not what's best for the people of the state, but how it will make them look. ...

"When she's in a room with you and she leaves the room to meet with the press, it's not show time. She's the same person outside that room as she was inside it."

"We went through a fairly extensive modeling exercise and detailed analysis of different types of structures on a gross with a variety of different adjustment mechanisms to them, always trying to recognize the administrative burden associated with each one and long-story-short, we would have to take a gross-based tax system and make so many adjustments to it that the administrative burden—and risk, basically on the state—would be just as high if not higher than if we just went to the net-based system," he said.

Under the final plan, Alaska's Clear and Equitable Share, or ACES, Galvin said the state would have a "gross tax-based safety net for revenues when prices dipped too low, while maintaining the full benefit of a net-based system that would provide a greater share of value from our oil and gas resources while still spurring new investment."

ACES, he said, also included a number of needed tools for protecting the state's interests in light of the net-based approach, such as bringing in industry class auditors.

Humor while under stress

On April 19, 2007, the Department of Revenue released its annual revenue forecast, telling Alaska lawmakers that they would have less money to spend in fiscal year 2008 than they expected due to a revised estimate of North Slope oil production and fewer tax dollars coming in under the new Petroleum Production Tax.

Revenue's forecast predicted the state would bring in $364 million less than expected in the next fiscal year, which would begin July 1. Lawmakers said the trend could also mean the state would be spending more than it earned by fiscal year 2009, as oil production on the North Slope was expected to continue to decline.

"I thought the oil fairy would save us again in '09 but what we are finding is that it isn't. And as we move up and down we are going to find we are in a deficit situation," Sen. Gary Wilken, R-Fairbanks, told the Associated Press.

ACES' hearings in Juneau intense

ACES, a hybrid of a gross and net tax system, would increase the tax rate to 25 percent from 22.5 percent, as well as create a more substantial floor in the event of low prices—10 percent of profits from the big Prudhoe Bay and Kuparuk fields — in the event of low oil prices.

The major North Slope oil and gas producers as well as non-facility and pipeline owners told legislators during the 30-day special session that began Oct. 18, 2007, that increasing the tax rate would put marginal projects at risk. The issue was the volume of oil production.

They argued that the easier barrels from existing oil deposits have been produced and that remaining resources in the big fields—in the tens of billions of barrels—include not just smaller accumulations of light oil but also more-expensive-to-produce heavy oil which was largely not yet being produced.

It would require more investment to keep barrels flowing down the trans-Alaska oil pipeline, the companies had argued, and many of those investments were marginal or somewhat marginal and at risk of not being funded if taxes were raised because competitive projects elsewhere would show better expected rates of return.

Public comment included those who believed the oil companies had made "obscene" profits in Alaska and that the state, as the resource owner, should get a bigger share of the proceeds from current high prices.

Get production back up

The oilfield service firms that provided Alaskans with a chunk of the state's highest paying jobs also communicated with state legislators, cautioning them against another oil production tax hike.

James Gilbert, president of Alaska-based Udelhoven Oilfield Systems Service, summed up the concerns of many of the contractors in a Nov. 14, 2007 Anchorage Daily News guest editorial.

Jim Gilbert

"We should not be considering raising taxes. We should be considering what it will take to get (oil) production back up to 2 million barrels per day," Gilbert wrote, noting his company provided 538 jobs in Alaska.

If the Legislature passed Palin's production tax plan it would prove that Alaska was "an unstable place to operate and invest," Gilbert said, noting that it had only been "14 months since the last tax increase was imposed."

Now that Alaska oil producers "are finally getting some payback for all those years of investments, we seem to hear nothing but complaints, accusations and whining," Gilbert said.

"No other industry—not fishing, not tourism, not mining, and certainly not the public sector—contributes what our employees, our clients or our clients' employees do," he said. "My clients (the oil companies) pay their 'fair share,' and they've been paying it for 30-plus years.

"We need to be looking at how we can get the pipeline back to

Gas reserves tax rides again!

A group of state lawmakers have revived a measure to tax Alaska natural gas reserves.

The measure, called the Alaska Gasline Now! Act, could appear on ballots in 2010, and is nearly identical to one filed several years ago. That measure failed.

There are two possible gas lines in the works, but potential pipeline builders have been talking about moving toward an open season "for the last decade or so," one of the sponsors, Rep. Harry Crawford, D-Anchorage, told Petroleum News on Sept. 29, 2008. "Show me, don't tell me," Crawford said.

Read the rest of the story at
http://www.petroleumnews.com/pnads/414745349.shtml

its operating capacity, not trying to tax the final 600,000 barrels per day into ultimate submission," Gilbert said.

Taxes under the current production profits tax, or PPT, were "considerably more than our profits" in 2006, BP Exploration (Alaska) President Doug Suttles said. BP's taxes to the state and federal governments on its Alaska assets totaled more than $2.7 billion for 2006. If ACES was passed as written, he said, it would be a 400 percent tax increase in a two-year period for oil and gas companies doing business in the state.

ACES passes

An expected Nov. 16 knuckle-biter finish to the 30-day special session never materialized.

A rewritten ACES passed in a form that was close enough to what the governor had asked for to satisfy her.

"We're happy with this bill," Palin said at a Nov. 16 press conference, and thanked legislators for their teamwork in gaining its passage. She said the bill met the three requirements the administration had when it started out: "We wanted to receive an equitable share for our resources, of course; also to maintain a positive investment climate; and to gain the tools needed to protect the state's interest and manage a net tax."

The possibility of negatively impacting oil and gas investment in Alaska worried House Speaker John Harris, R-Valdez, who voted for the bill: "The governor and her administration have crafted a bill and pushed it through the Legislature that will either tap the producers for another $1.5 billion without harm, or end up hurting our economy by driving away oil industry investment. We will need billions of dollars of investment to keep our production up, so I am hopeful the governor has not made a serious mistake with this legislation. But we won't really know for sure for a couple of years."

A GLANCE FORWARD

Sarah Palin: Alaska superstar

Gov. Sarah Palin was aided in her efforts to change the state's relationship with the oil and gas industry by an unprecedented popularity among the Alaska public.

Palin won her campaign for governor with 48 percent of the vote, but quickly earned approval ratings much higher, finding support from Democrats and Republicans alike. Marc Hellenthal, an Anchorage-based pollster, said Palin's popularity as governor—judged by the percent of Alaskans with positive feelings toward her—was simply unbelievable.

"We've been polling 25 years in the state, and nobody had even come close to an 80-percent positive," he said.

Before her nomination as John McCain's running mate at the end of August, Palin's approval ratings ranged from 79 to 86 percent, according to Hellenthal's figures. Of all the governors, lawmakers, mayors, and other public figures Hellenthal had tracked, only two had reached 70 percent.

State lawmakers say Palin's popularity probably helped her win support in the Legislature for her gas pipeline legislation – the

Alaska Gasline Inducement Act—and rewrite of the state's oil production tax.

"It certainly had a bearing," said House Speaker John Harris, a Republican from Valdez. "It might have been a significant bearing at one point in time."

Democrats were generally inclined to support the initiatives, which were opposed by the industry, Harris said, but some Republicans were probably swayed by their desire to support the Republican governor.

Harris added that if Palin had not been so popular, her initiatives probably would have had less support and might not have passed at all.

"I don't know what the numbers would have been," he said. "Not everyone was real enthusiastic with the AGIA situation, but it was what we had to deal with."

Palin's AGIA bill passed the legislature with only one vote against it. (The vote to award a license under AGIA to TransCanada was more divided.)

Rep. David Guttenberg, a Democrat from Fairbanks, said it was much harder to speak out against Palin's proposals than against those of her predecessor, Gov. Frank Murkowski, whose approval ratings tumbled to less than 30 percent by the end of his term, prompting him to joke in a 2006 campaign ad that he might well need a "personality transplant."

"If [Palin] didn't have that high rating," Guttenberg said, "she would have had a lot more trouble doing what she was doing."

Impact of her popularity felt in Legislature

Palin didn't use her popularity to pressure lawmakers directly, Guttenberg and others say, but the impact was still felt. Sen. Gene Therriault, a Republican from North Pole, said the popularity of Palin's proposals also pressured lawmakers to support them.

The governor's popularity among the general public was not always reflected in the Capitol. Therriault and Guttenberg, who both supported the governor's proposals, described lawmakers' feelings toward her as mixed.

"She's very nice and personable, but she didn't work with us," Guttenberg said. "That was difficult."

Many lawmakers were irked by Palin's unexpected budget vetoes and by what they described as a lack of communication.

Palin's popularity took a dive in the state after she joined the McCain campaign, according to multiple polls. Hellenthal and others attributed the drop to the partisan nature of the campaign and the chilling effect on support from Democrats.

But Hellenthal added that she was still the most popular public figure in the state and would likely remain so if McCain lost and Palin returned to Alaska as governor.

"It's kind of like somebody going to the big leagues and then coming back home," he said. "She wouldn't suffer."

—by Stefan Milkowski, for Sarah takes on Big Oil

"Chief among those (AGIA) principles is access for all gas explorers; expansion assured for companies with new gas volumes; a reasonable and hopefully very low tariff structure; and moving the gas pipeline project forward expeditiously."

—Marty Rutherford

Chapter 10

Applications in, gas remains an issue

"Your leadership and that of your administration has been outstanding and your integrity and transparent style are a breath of fresh air in what has proven to be a rather shady and smoke-filled past in regard to energy issues in Alaska."

—David Sokol, chairman and CEO of MidAmerican Holdings Co.

By Kristen Nelson

Gov. Sarah Palin's Alaska Gasline Inducement Act passed the Alaska Legislature in May 2007, and on July 2 her gas line team posted the request for applications on the AGIA Web site, officially kicking off the application process. Applications were due to the state Oct. 1, a deadline later extended—at the request of potential applicants—to Nov. 30.

On Nov. 30 the state announced it had received five AGIA applications; it also received a non-AGIA application from ConocoPhillips.

The AGIA applications were from AEnergia LLC; the Alaska Gasline Port Authority; the Alaska Natural Gas Development Authority; a joint application from Little Susitna Construction Co. and Sinopec ZPEB; and a joint application from TransCanada and Foothills Pipelines. (See stories on AEnergia and Little Susitna-Sinopec at end of chapter.)

Palin called it "an exciting day for Alaska and really a very exciting time for Americans." She said with AGIA the state was working to address "Alaska's rising energy costs" and the nation's energy needs.

"Today's progress, under AGIA, demonstrates to the world that Alaska is well on our way to bringing this long sought after and necessary infrastructure, a natural gas pipeline, to fruition."

159

Although no North Slope producers applied under AGIA, Palin said that "doesn't mean that they cannot be participants in this gas line. Once a licensee was chosen, Alaska's best partner, then a third-party partner would no doubt be attracted also by the licensee," she said.

The ConocoPhillips' proposal was outside AGIA, and Palin said the state was "committed to AGIA." She said the companies that submitted applications under AGIA were "not stalking horses," and said she hoped they would spur interest by the producers. The administration would look at the ConocoPhillips proposal, Palin said, "and we'll hear them out but they won't be considered under this AGIA process."

ConocoPhillips application outside AGIA

Department of Natural Resources Deputy Commissioner Marty Rutherford, the gas team leader, said the administration had said from the first discussions of AGIA with the Legislature that even if the producers chose not to participate under the gasline inducement act, "we are convinced that these world-class corporations will in fact ship gas when they know what the construction costs and the tariff structure will be."

The producers needed to monetize their North Slope gas and book the reserves, "and they need to honor their lease responsibilities to the State of Alaska," she said, which includes the obligation to move the state's "resource to market when it's economic to do so."

Those applying under AGIA indicated their willingness to satisfy the state's requirements, Rutherford said: "Chief among those principles are access for all gas explorers; expansion assured for companies with new gas volumes; a reasonable and hopefully very low tariff structure; and moving the gas pipeline project forward expeditiously."

Compared to the Stranded Gas Development Act process under the Murkowski administration, "we have identified what requirements are necessary in a gas pipeline to ensure Alaska's long-term economic interests." Under AGIA, she said, "our long-term financial interests and the nation's interests in getting gas to market are protected by these must haves, these commercial elements."

The first step in the AGIA process was a review of applications to make sure they had been responsive to AGIA requirements. Then the applications would be posted on the Internet and public comments solicited on the complete applications.

The comments and the applications would be reviewed and complete applications analyzed on the basis of net present value to the state and the likelihood of success, "which means fundamentally that the applicants can in fact deliver the project they have indicated they're proposing," Rutherford said.

The in-state entities that applied

Two in-state entities were among the applicants: the Alaska Gasline Port Authority and the Alaska Natural Gas Development Authority.

The port authority, a joint venture of the North Slope Borough, the Fairbanks North Star Borough and the City of Valdez, was established in 1999 in support of a liquefied natural gas project.

JUDY PATRICK

Jim Whitaker

Palin had supported this proposal during her run for governor. The port authority plan would provide natural gas along its line—which would parallel the trans-Alaska oil pipeline from the North Slope to Valdez—and export natural gas as LNG.

The port authority's "mission, since day one, has been focused on bringing the maximum benefits of North Slope gas development to the people of Alaska in the form of access to gas, greater competition in the development of gas, new and expanded value added industries throughout the state and jobs for Alaskans," Jim Whitaker, mayor of the Fairbanks North Star Borough and chairman of the port authority's board, said in a statement after the port authority application was turned in.

ANGDA, a state entity established by statewide voter initiative, was originally also focused on an LNG project out of Valdez, but took on ensuring that natural gas reached Alaska consumers, both along the main gas pipeline and in other areas of the state.

The ANGDA proposal, a spur line (smaller diameter pipeline that would take its gas from the larger gas line that would go into Canada) to Southcentral Alaska, was designed to accompany a mainline application.

TransCanada, Foothills involved since 1970s

Although TransCanada and Foothills had been involved in efforts to build an Alaska gas pipeline since the 1970s, their AGIA application was no sure thing.

Tony Palmer, vice president of Alaska business development for TransCanada, told legislators during AGIA hearings that TransCanada was not comfortable with the AGIA requirement to proceed beyond a failed open season (not enough gas committed at an open season to fill a line) through a Federal Energy Regulatory Commission certificate.

Palin administration officials said the requirement to proceed beyond a failed open season was crucial to ensure that the North Slope producers couldn't kill the project by not committing gas in an initial open season.

Palmer told legislators in early 2007 that monies spent after a failed open season to get a FERC certificate "are truly at risk if the project does not proceed."

He said it wasn't just the money, since people would have to be dedicated to the project and it would "take a significant dedication of our corporation's talent to pursue the project."

TransCanada held the rights granted for the original North Slope gas pipeline, and as such had a 30-year history with the project, Palmer told legislators in March 2007.

The non-applicants include MidAmerican

One application the state did not get was from MidAmerican Energy Holdings Co., which had testified on AGIA and had been involved in attempts to move a gas pipeline forward under the Murkowski administration.

In a Nov. 30 letter to the governor, David Sokol, the company's chairman and chief executive officer, referred to the corruption scandal gripping the state when he said "the deepening and ongoing investigations into political and corporate corruption in Alaska make a thorough and thoughtful proposal in compliance with AGIA an unrealistic exercise for our organization."

Sokol told Palin he did not consider her administration to be the problem: "... your leadership and that of your administration has been outstanding and your integrity and transparent style are a breath of fresh air in what has proven to be a rather shady and smoke-filled past in regard to energy issues in Alaska."

MidAmerican applied in 2004 to build an Alaska gas pipeline project under the Stranded Gas Development Act, but later withdrew its application in a dispute with the Murkowski administration over exclusive development rights for the project.

MidAmerican had proposed that the state reimburse it for half of its estimated $100 million in development costs for the project; Gov. Frank Murkowski declined.

MidAmerican then proposed that instead of reimbursement, the state grant it a three-year exclusive right to build the pipeline, later extended to five years.

In March 2007, Kirk Morgan, president of MidAmerican subsidiary Kern River Gas Transmission Co., told Senate Resources: "We felt like, frankly, we were a stalking horse to create leverage for the last administration. And we're not coming up here to go through another beauty contest."

Morgan said that alignment with both the state and the producers would be necessary for a successful project; MidAmerican would go ahead with project work while the state settled alignment issues with the producers, he said.

He also said that while MidAmerican did not ask the state for the $500 million in state matching funds included in AGIA, "The alignment that the $500 million creates is extremely important," and not just to MidAmerican: "It's an important signal to the marketplace; it gives the project much more credibility."

LNG the way, says BG

BG Group, one of Anadarko Petroleum's exploration partners in the gas-prone Brooks Range Foothills, had not submitted an AGIA application, but in a Nov. 29, 2007, letter to Palin, Martin Houston, BG Group's executive vice president and managing director, said BG remained "extremely interested" in participating in bringing Alaska gas to market.

"We remain staunch supporters of your efforts to launch a transparent and competitive process that guarantees access to pipeline capacity for Alaska's new explorers," he wrote.

Houston said BG had worked on options with the intention of bidding under AGIA and believed "more than ever, that a major infrastructure project is economic and will be developed."

"However, given the number of moving parts around all aspects of the project, there was still too much economic uncertainty for us at this stage," to submit an AGIA application.

Houston told the governor that based on the work it had done, BG believed "that LNG should and will be part of the solution for the future development of Alaska's natural gas resources."

Liquefied natural gas could be an anchor project or part of a larger highway project, he said. In addition to providing in-state gas and revenues to the state, Houston said LNG would allow the state "to benefit from market diversification and the flexibility to target the highest value markets at any given time."

BG was the largest supplier of LNG to the United States and

supplied almost 50 percent of LNG imported to the United States in 2006, David Keane, BG's vice president policy and corporate affairs for North America, Caribbean and global LNG, told the Arctic Energy Summit Technology Conference in Anchorage in October 2007.

ConocoPhillips wants fiscal terms

Jim Mulva, ConocoPhillips chairman and CEO, told Palin in a Nov. 30 letter accompanying the company's non-AGIA application that the company was "prepared to make signifi-cant investments, without state matching funds, to advance the natural gas pipeline project towards our shared objective of seeing the conclusion of a successful open season within 36 months."

Jim Mulva

While the company didn't want the state's money, and was willing to meet a number of the requirements in AGIA, it wanted something AGIA didn't offer—natural gas fiscal terms for shippers making commit-ments in the initial open season.

Fiscal certainty, including the 45-year freeze on tax and royalty rates, was one of the issues that had blocked legislative approval of the contract former Gov. Murkowski struck in 2006 with BP, ConocoPhillips and ExxonMobil. Legislators said the Murkowski deal also raised sovereignty and constitutional issues.

BP, Conoco and Exxon and their supporters in Alaska's business community had campaigned hard for what they described as a more flexible bill, telling legislators that the AGIA bill did not adequately address fiscal certainty and required applicants for the AGIA license to meet specific requirements.

The companies had told legislators they wanted the state to give applicants an opportunity to say how they would respond to general goals, rather than requiring applicants to meet specific require-ments.

The companies had also said that fiscal terms covering the whole range of state take from the industry would have to be negotiated.

All three of the companies told legislators before the bill was passed that they would not be able to make applications which conformed to AGIA requirements.

ConocoPhillips described its proposal as giving the state a choice: "This proposal provides an alternative path forward for the ANS gas pipeline project which is, in our view, the most certain way to create a vibrant and successful development effort for the project."

The company said the pipeline shippers would be "be required to bear the burdens of multi-billion dollar financial commitments" through their long-term ship-or-pay commitments. Because of that, "a natural gas pipeline development effort would only be sustainable and ultimately successful if there is recognition of the need for an appropriate balance of risk and reward among the pipeline owners, the state and the producers and prospective shippers."

Getting gas into the pipeline

With six options on its plate at the end of 2007, the state would ultimately move ahead on only one (see Chapter 11).

But another issue remained unresolved: getting gas into a line.

If the passage of AGIA and the receipt of AGIA applications was a step toward getting a gas pipeline from Alaska's North Slope to market, getting the volumes of gas to fill that line for a period of years was also necessary.

For the line to move forward, gas had to be contractually committed, long-term, by the owners.

While at least a couple hundred trillion cubic feet of natural gas have been estimated by the federal government to occur onshore and offshore Alaska's North Slope, only proven reserves were of immediate use for a gas pipeline because of uncertainties associated with discovering and developing additional natural gas accumulations.

Those drilled and delineated reserves would have to be committed by the leaseholders—primarily BP, ConocoPhillips and ExxonMobil—who have said they required fiscal concessions from the state before they would commit gas, and have also said ownership in a gas line was necessary because that was the only way they could control pipeline construction costs, and by extension the tariff.

Further complicating the picture, in April 2008 BP and ConocoPhillips announced that they had formed a joint venture to build their own gas pipeline, Denali—The Alaska Gas Pipeline (see Chapter 11).

Would Big 3 commit gas?

The issue of whether Alaska's Big 3 oil and gas companies would commit natural gas to an AGIA-backed TransCanada Alaska project was raised at the May 22, 2008, press conference announcing the administration's decision to recommend an AGIA license for the TransCanada Alaska project.

Palin said there was no reason major oil producers wouldn't want to commit their gas to such an economic project "that will provide them such huge profits."

"They're reasonable commercial players; they are competitors; certainly they are looking out for their bottom line. There is no reason for them to hesitate, we believe, when the line is ready to go. When they see the commitment to actually construct the line there is no reason for them to not fulfill the mandates of their shareholders and that is to boost their bottom line and that is what they'll be able to do by committing their gas."

The governor said "the market is going to dictate" the amount of gas the producers would commit. "It wouldn't make any sense for them to hesitate to put their gas in the line."

Palin said the state always had the option of litigating, "making sure that oil producers are abiding by the provisions in their leases," especially leases that have been "held for so many years now without the level of production that Alaskans and Americans need."

But the state doesn't want to litigate "right out of the chute," she said.

Issue of success

Commissioner of Revenue Pat Galvin said the administration "looked very closely at the issue of how to get gas and whether it's reasonably likely that the TransCanada project would end up with gas commitments." TransCanada Alaska's AGIA application was evaluated on the net present value of cash flow to the state weighted by the likelihood of a project's success.

Galvin said a big part of whether the TransCanada project would get gas commitments was based on "ensuring that it's an economic project and that it will provide a good return" to companies committing gas to the line. The evaluations the administration ran showed that there would be a good return, he said.

And with the BP-ConocoPhillips Denali project the producers had given themselves a choice, Galvin said: They could choose between TransCanada and Denali, with the Denali project providing them "with some leverage on TransCanada, on the state," so it was clearly in the state's interest to ensure the TransCanada project was attractive to the producers.

Galvin said the state would continue to analyze TransCanada's project "to determine if there's things that the state needs to do to enhance the attractiveness of the TransCanada project" in order to get those gas commitments from the Big 3 North Slope producers.

Rutherford noted that AGIA already had upstream incentives that would be valuable to the producers associated with royalty terms—both the state's rights to switch between taking gas in-kind or in-value and how the gas is valued, and "commitments on the part of the State of Alaska to not change the fiscal structure on production tax for 10 years if they participate in that (first binding) open season."

Why wouldn't they want to sell?

"How do you get them to sell the gas if they don't want to? So why would they not want to?" Galvin asked in a September 2008 interview.

If the producers don't show up at an open season the question will be asked: Why didn't they show up?

"And we'll be just as curious as everybody else and we'll want to know, is there something that the state needed to do that was a reasonable request on the part of the companies that was a legitimate reason not to commit their gas to the line?"

Galvin said he meant something the companies had to have, not something they wished they had.

If the companies didn't commit gas at an open season the state would be asking why not, he said. And the state expected others would also be asking that question, including members of Congress, Lower 48 consumers, utilities companies and the producers' shareholders.

The state's analysis (as part of the TransCanada AGIA application evaluation) showed that the North Slope producers would make "billions of dollars" by shipping their gas through a TransCanada line, he said.

They have the opportunity to do much better than the state calculated because the "cost estimates (for the pipeline) that TransCanada gave us were significantly lower than what we ran all of our economics on" because the state's estimates were run on the midpoint of its scenarios, Galvin said.

AGIA critics don't ask right questions

Critics of AGIA appeared to stop at 'what if the producers don't commit gas to TransCanada' and assumed the state's next step is to sue, leading to the conclusion that AGIA "is a litigation strategy," he said.

Galvin said the state doesn't expect to sue the North Slope producers because it doesn't expect them to breach their leases.

The state doesn't expect them to forego the billions they could earn selling the gas and fight the state "just out of principle."

The Big 3 didn't operate that way, he said. "They're going to look at it as a commercial opportunity. Our analysis tells us it's going to be a very attractive commercial opportunity for them."

A lot of analysis before open season

A lot of analysis would be done between now and the open season for the gas pipeline, he said, including analysis of the will of the state to provide some concessions: Would the state eventually relent and provide concessions? Galvin said the companies could go through another election cycle and be successful in bringing in members of the Legislature who would be more sympathetic to their view.

It was reasonable to expect that those things would play into the producers' strategy, he said.

It wasn't just an economic numbers game, Galvin said. "This is game theory: ... If this person does this, what's this person going to do in response to that? And then what's the other person—this third person—going to do in response. ...

"And what's the state going to be able to do in response to the position of these other three?"

Then you go back and ask what if this person does something different? What would the response to that be?

"And you have to imagine all of these different scenarios and think about OK, what is the role of the state today and for the next two years? And it's to continually assess where the players are, where the opportunity is to get forward movement, where the opportunity for the state is to provide something that may smooth the way without costing the state too much."

Will the state concede?

"And to what extent does the state just need to show the resolve that says, you know, we're not the softest side here that you can get more value out of, because part of what we've seen is that the companies hold out from actual forward movement simply to see if the state concedes and we end up with forward movement from the companies simply by being resolute in our position," Galvin said.

The commissioner noted that he's said publicly that the state didn't know where AGIA played out. ... "The structure of AGIA ... the concept behind AGIA is we know what the state needs to do now to get this project moving forward. And we know that through AGIA we're going to be at a decision point between now and the open season for the state to make another decision on whether or not we're going to throw anything else into the kitty before the open season starts."

There was no obligation on the state's part to do anything further "because we've allowed the commercial forces to move this project to the next decision point," Galvin said.

"But the state will have every opportunity before that to make another decision and once we get to that open season, and we see where everybody positions themselves, then we'll have every opportunity to make another decision about what we're going to do."

And the state would have better information at that point and be able to make a better decision than it could now, "and we'll leave less money on the table than what we would if we did what Murkowski did, basically turn over the store for the purposes of avoiding any ... potential conflict, but then forget the second part, which is get an obligation, get a commitment, in response," he said.

The regulator: AOGCC

In addition to the issue of getting commitments of gas in an open season, there was the issue of how much gas can be committed to a gas pipeline before there was an unacceptable loss of Prudhoe Bay oil production.

Prudhoe Bay held the majority of known natural gas reserves on the North Slope and that natural gas, produced along with crude oil, was reinjected into the reservoir. The reinjected gas maintained the reservoir pressure necessary for oil production and was used in various enhanced oil recovery projects which had greatly increased crude oil recovery from Prudhoe Bay.

When production began from the field in 1977 it was estimated that some 9 billion barrels of crude oil would be recovered; as of the end of 2007, more than 11 billion barrels had been recovered from the field; it was estimated that the field would produce a total of 13 billion barrels, and production was expected to continue for a number of years.

While getting Prudhoe Bay natural gas into a gas sales pipeline required the leaseholders at Prudhoe to commit to ship that gas, there was also a regulatory requirement.

Offtake rates—the volumes that could be produced from a field—were regulated in Alaska by the Alaska Oil and Gas Conservation Commission, a quasi-judicial state agency that Palin once chaired (see chapter 3).

All U.S. states with oil or gas production had similar agencies, which ensured that recovery from fields was done at rates which maximized total recovery over time.

In the early days of oil production competing companies drilled competing wells to get at the oil based on a principle of first-come first-served, called the rule of capture, and too-rapid production dropped reservoir pressures so rapidly that only small percentages of oil could be recovered.

State governments stepped in to regulate production rates and to protect the rights of adjacent leaseholders, prohibiting a leaseholder from drilling diagonally to reach under an adjacent lease to drain a neighbor's hydrocarbon.

The Alaska Oil and Gas Conservation Commission, or AOGCC, established a gas offtake rate at Prudhoe Bay in the late 1970s when oil production began. While a North Slope natural gas pipeline carrying some 4 billion to 4.5 billion cubic feet a day of natural gas is generally discussed, the current offtake rate, the allowable withdrawal of natural gas from Prudhoe Bay for sale, has not been changed and is still less than 3 bcf a day.

Gas used to recover oil

The natural gas at Prudhoe Bay was used to maintain reservoir pressure and to increase oil recovery.

Cathy Foerster, the engineering commissioner on the three-member AGOCC, told legislators in 2007 that while some 34.5 trillion cubic feet of natural gas were known at Prudhoe Bay and Point Thomson (an undeveloped field to the east of Prudhoe), "very few people realize that hundreds of millions of barrels of oil and condensate could be lost if gas off-take from these fields is not correctly managed."

JUDY PATRICK

Cathy Foerster

Using natural gas to maintain reservoir pressure increased oil recovery "but producing gas depletes reservoir pressure. ... Gas reserves in most fields are usually sold only after the liquid hydrocarbon reserves have been depleted," Foerster said.

Until the liquids were depleted gas was reinjected to provide energy to produce the liquids or for enhanced oil recovery. "Both of those things are happening right now at Prudhoe Bay and the other North Slope fields," she said.

In January 2008, Foerster told the Senate Resources Committee that two of the commission's missions, preventing hydrocarbon waste and encouraging ultimate hydrocarbon recovery, had come into play in gas discussions.

Foerster said ultimate recovery from Prudhoe Bay was now expected to reach 13 billion barrels. The reservoir didn't grow, she said, addressing the difference between the original estimated recovery of some 9 billion barrels and the 13 billion barrels now expected. The field's owners had made investments and there had been technological advances, both of which contributed to the fact that the owners now expected to recover some 60 percent of the field's oil, compared to the base level of 20-25 percent recovered at most reservoirs.

Prudhoe has estimated 24.5 tcf

Prudhoe Bay gas was estimated at about 24.5 trillion cubic feet (the majority of the remainder of the 35 tcf of proven North Slope natural gas reserves, some 8 tcf by state estimates, were found at Point Thomson; several fields had smaller gas accumulations).

Some 7 billion to 8 billion cubic feet a day of gas was produced at Prudhoe along with oil and water. The oil is separated from the gas and water, both of which were reinjected.

"So that oil rim that's in the middle is being squeezed from below and above—below by the water and above by the gas—to keep the pressure high enough so that the oil can continue to flow," Foerster said.

Because gas was being used to maintain reservoir pressure, "The later we start to sell the gas, and the more aggressively BP (the Prudhoe Bay field operator) has been in producing the oil in the meantime, the less oil will be left in the reservoir at risk of being lost to decreased pressure or other reservoir mechanisms associated with selling the gas," she said.

The commission sets gas offtake rules and the rate for Prudhoe, 2.7 bcf a day, was set in 1977. The commission would have to approve a request for a larger offtake rate and had already undertaken studies to provide information for that decision, one which the commission would make when the Prudhoe Bay field operator requested a change in gas offtake rate.

Foerster said AOGCC was working "to help prepare the state for the eventual sale of our North Slope gas resource." The state would want to sell whatever volume was needed from Prudhoe Bay, and sell that when it was needed to ensure a gas line proceeds, she said. What the commission would require was that the Prudhoe Bay operator "aggressively produces as much oil and puts in place as much mitigation for losses as possible before the gas sales begin."

BP had been aggressively producing the oil using horizontal

extended-reach multilateral wells, by injecting water into the gas cap and by enhanced oil recovery. Assuming BP continued to accelerate oil production, avoided "major unplanned shutdowns" and developed and implemented "strategies to mitigate oil losses" then "by the time we get a gas line, the oil volumes left at risk at Prudhoe Bay ... will not be sufficient to derail a gas pipeline," she said.

Point Thomson more complicated

Point Thomson was not a developed field—estimates of the reserves there were from exploration wells drilled in the 1970s and 1980s. There was insufficient data from Point Thomson to allow AOGCC to make an offtake rate decision.

There were also legal issues at Point Thomson.

The Alaska Department of Natural Resources terminated the Point Thomson unit in 2006 and revoked the leases because it could not get the Point Thomson operator, ExxonMobil Production Co., to commit to field development.

ExxonMobil and the other leaseholders appealed DNR's decision in state court and subsequently submitted a pilot development plan to test cycling at Point Thomson.

If ExxonMobil and the other existing owners win in court they would develop the field; the state could win and re-offer the Point Thomson acreage for lease and the company or companies placing the largest bids for the acreage would then have the right to develop the field.

Whether the field had old or new owners, AOGCC still needed to make a gas offtake ruling for Point Thomson.

Thomson classified as an oil field

Foerster had told legislators that Point Thomson, commonly referred to as a gas field, was what was called in engineering terms "a gas condensate reservoir or a retrograde condensate reservoir." The reservoir was at very high pressure—about twice that of the Prudhoe Bay reservoir—and liquid hydrocarbons existed as gases.

Under AOGCC regulations, Point Thomson was an oil field, so AOGCC would have to approve a gas offtake rate—a rate that maximized recovery and minimized waste.

Foerster said the way to achieve greater ultimate recovery and prevent waste when producing a gas condensate reservoir was to cycle the gas and remove the liquids before selling the gas.

The pilot cycling plan proposed by ExxonMobil would produce condensate to the surface. Liquids would be stripped out and shipped in a pipeline built to connect to an existing line which tied into the trans-Alaska oil pipeline.

The remaining gas would be re-pressurized and injected back into the reservoir, keeping up reservoir pressure so that liquids didn't drop out in the reservoir where they would not be recoverable.

Foerster said estimates of recoverable liquids at Point Thomson ranged from 200 million to 400 million barrels. While you could look at that as a small loss to get 8 tcf of gas, she said, "we have time, right now, to be developing Point Thomson, cycling the gas and recovering those liquids," allowing recovery of liquids now and gas once a gas pipeline is in place.

Forester said—in January 2008—that there was time now to develop Point Thomson with a cycling project which would produce the oil and recycle the gas. "But the longer Point Thomson remains undeveloped the less time we will have."

She said she didn't know the economics at Point Thomson.

"I don't know that there's a profit to be made on the oil; all I know is that the physics say that the only way to get the majority of that oil is to cycle."

Reprinted from the Dec. 9, 2007, issue of Petroleum News

AEnergia not new
to Alaska gas line

Burkhard says North Slope pipeline would
go to Calgary AECO hub, and support ancillary
line to Kenai or Valdez, including LNG

By Kay Cashman
Petroleum News

One of the five proposals received under the Alaska Gasline Inducement Act to build a gas pipeline from Alaska's North Slope came from AEnergia, a recently formed Alaska limited liability corporation with a Sacramento, Calif., address.

While the LLC might be new, its members have been working on getting a gas pipeline built since 2001under the joint venture name of GSS/TC.

But the experience of AEnergia's members with an Alaska gas line proposal dates back much further than that. During the original effort to build an Alaska natural gas pipeline in the late 1970s and early 1980s, AEnergia core members were working for the consulting firms that provided the earth sciences design expertise.

AEnergia executive Bill Burkhard told Petroleum News in 2003 that by "project's end, we had completed about 70 percent of the alignment geology, 50 percent of the surface and groundwater hydrology, 30 percent of the geotechnical engineering including thermal modeling and climatology, and a substantial portion of the environmental work." ....

Read more: www.petroleumnews.com/pnads/195630182.shtml

Reprinted from the Dec. 9, 2007, issue of Petroleum News

Chinese bidder faces political hurdles

Sinopec has pipeline expertise, financial muscle, but it does business in many politically unpopular places

By Allen Baker

For Petroleum News

The surprise pipeline bid from a subsidiary of China's Sinopec could provide an interesting new link between Alaska and Asia's mainland. But it's unlikely to get out of the starting gate due to an impressive load of political baggage.

The formal bid comes from Sinopec's oil services subsidiary, Sinopec Zhongyuan Petroleum Exploration Bureau, along with Little Susitna Construction Co. of Anchorage, founded by Hong Kong-born Dominic S.F. Lee, P.E., in 1980. Little Susitna Construction has substantial credentials as an Alaska engineering, design and construction management firm, participating in more than 500 Alaska projects including design work for the Service High School swimming pool and some North Slope facilities back in the ARCO days. But there's not much oil industry connection. ....

Read the rest of the story online at:
www.petroleumnews.com/pnads/680943279.shtml

"Without AGIA's requirements, we'd be leveraged by a small group of companies. We can't surrender revenue, judicial process and our sovereignty."

—Gov. Sarah Palin in Jan. 15, 2008, state-of-the-state address

Chapter 11

Palin gets TransCanada AGIA license approved

LNG "is not dead, not by any stretch of the imagination." ... an LNG project would work in conjunction with TransCanada, and approving the TransCanada proposal "is actually the best way to keep LNG alive," because if demand is high enough, TransCanada would ship gas for an LNG project, down a Y-line to Prince William Sound.

—Gov. Sarah Palin

By Kristen Nelson

Passage of the TransCanada AGIA license put Alaska Gov. Sarah Palin three-for-three on her administration's big oil and gas initiatives: passage in 2007 of the Alaska Gasline Inducement Act, AGIA, and production tax increases in ACES, Alaska's Clear and Equitable Share, and the 2008 approval of the TransCanada AGIA license.

The fight to the finish on approval of the TransCanada AGIA license was a long one, lasting the better part of three months. It wasn't until Aug. 1, 2008, one day before the deadline for approval, that Palin's proposal for awarding a license to TransCanada under AGIA was passed by the Alaska Legislature.

AGIA provided matching funds and other inducements in return for the gas pipeline Palin wanted. The bill establishing AGIA had passed with just one nay vote in May 2007.

By May 2008, however, the Legislature's Republican leadership no longer favored AGIA and fought approval of the TransCanada AGIA license.

The 2007 to 2008 change appeared driven by a lingering desire for a liquefied natural gas project, the so-called all-Alaska line, and by the April 2008 unveiling of a joint venture between BP and

ConocoPhillips to build a line, the Denali project.

TransCanada only complete application

On Nov. 30, 2007, the State of Alaska had six applications for an Alaska natural gas pipeline project, five under AGIA and one from ConocoPhillips that was outside of AGIA.

By early 2008, that number had been winnowed to one: The state rejected the ConocoPhillips proposal to negotiate outside of AGIA and found only one of the five AGIA applications to be complete, that from TransCanada and Foothills.

Following its decision that the Alaska Gasline Port Authority AGIA application was incomplete, the administration broadened the AGIA review process to include liquefied natural gas.

The port authority had requested reconsideration of the decision, bringing to bear the political clout of former Gov. Wally Hickel, who had supported Palin in her run for governor, and Backbone II.

In a Jan. 30, 2008, letter, Commissioner of Revenue Pat Galvin and Commissioner of Natural Resources Tom Irwin told Bill Walker, general counsel for the Port Authority that the state would not reconsider its decision that the port authority AGIA application was incomplete.

They did commit, however, to evaluating LNG—the port authority had proposed an LNG project—before "determining whether a pipeline that goes through Canada will sufficiently maximize the benefits to the people of Alaska and merits issuance of a license."

Governor commits to comparison

Palin had earlier acknowledged the role of the port authority and the Alaska Natural Gas Development Authority in the gas pipeline project, saying: "They got this project off the dime."

"It's been these two Alaskan entities that have really helped kick start this process and this project and they're to be thanked for

Mission to reduce energy costs

The Palin administration's mission to reduce energy costs in Alaska mirrors, in many ways, some of the efforts to do the same on a national level. Two recent articles in Petroleum News introduce the Alaska Energy Authority and Alaska's energy coordinator, Steve Haagenson.

See "Palin names energy coordinator for Alaska, plans to immediately address crisis in rural areas" in March 9, 2008, issue of Petroleum News at www.petroleumnews.com/pnads/984396447.shtml and "State to host energy town hall meetings" in May 4, 2008, issue of Petroleum News at www.petroleumnews.com/pnads/476816795.shtml.

For more information on AEA: www.akenergyauthority.org.

doing so. They've constantly reminded us to give everyone, via competition, a fair shot at this project," she said Jan. 4, 2008, in announcing that the only complete application was from TransCanada.

On Jan. 30, the governor wrote to Hickel and David Gottstein, co-chairmen of Backbone II, a citizens' watchdog group, promising an LNG evaluation. "My administration recognizes and shares your interest in a comparison of an 'overland route and a route to tidewater and LNG.' You are absolutely correct that this comparison is of critical importance to the state," the governor wrote.

The original Backbone, with Hickel as a member, formed in 1999 to oppose BP's acquisition of ARCO. The state, the Alaska Legislature, federal regulators—and Alaska residents—were concerned about the concentrating effect such a merger would have had on North Slope and trans-Alaska oil pipeline ownership; BP and ARCO were the two operators on the North Slope at that time and major pipeline owners.

Ultimately the Federal Trade Commission forced BP to divest ARCO's Alaska assets, which were purchased by Phillips Petroleum, now ConocoPhillips.

Backbone became involved in gas development issues in 2001, publishing a study urging the state to look broadly at gas development options.

The LNG evaluation

Palin told Hickel and Gottstein her administration would "undertake a detailed evaluation of likely LNG project designs before determining whether a pipeline that goes through Canada will sufficiently maximize the benefits to the people of Alaska and merits issuance of a license."

Alaska has an LNG facility on the Kenai Peninsula. It was the nation's first, and it has been exporting liquefied Cook Inlet natural gas to the Far East since 1969. A proposal to commercialize North Slope natural gas via an LNG project with a liquefaction facility in Valdez was one of the original proposals to export North Slope natural gas. Hickel is a long-time backer of an LNG project.

Palin supported the port authority project during her campaign for governor and as a result had been widely viewed as supporting the LNG option, referred to as the all-Alaska project because the gas pipeline would be entirely within the state. Some of the public comments on the TransCanada AGIA application criticized what was seen as a change in position by the governor, a number of people saying they voted for the governor believing she supported the all-Alaska line.

At a Jan. 30, 2008, press conference, Galvin said that in making the decision on the port authority application the state faced two issues: what to do within the AGIA process; and how an LNG project fit into an analysis of the TransCanada application. He said while the port authority application remained incomplete and the request for reconsideration was denied, the administration was committing to "fully evaluate" an LNG project compared to the TransCanada project.

The obligation under AGIA was to ensure that the best project moved forward and Galvin said he didn't think that could be done without a full airing of the LNG option.

Irwin said the LNG analysis would compare net present value to the state and the likelihood of success. The TransCanada application included an LNG option as an alternative if there were issues with the line through Canada or insufficient volumes of gas for a line into Canada, and he said it would be logical for legislators to ask if the administration had looked at LNG.

Galvin said the gas line team would put together the most competitive LNG project it could and said the administration needed to make sure that, if it goes forward with TransCanada, that it can tell Alaskans it is the best project for the state. To do that requires looking at an LNG option.

Conoco proposal rebuffed

The governor had earlier said thanks but no thanks to the ConocoPhillips alternative gas line proposal.

In a Jan. 9 letter to Jim Mulva, ConocoPhillips CEO, Palin said the ConocoPhillips alternative continued "the approach advanced by the producers in the Stranded Gas Development Act negotiations," and did not meet terms the Legislature established under AGIA.

Palin acknowledged that the ConocoPhillips proposal didn't seek the alternatives offered under AGIA, but said it "instead appears to require that the state change its fiscal system and concede crucial sovereign prerogatives in order for ConocoPhillips to agree to consider building a gas pipeline."

She said that under the stranded gas negotiations "these types of changes to the state's fiscal system would have deprived the state of its ability to regulate its oil and gas activities, including taxation, for 30 to 40 years and would have cost at least $10 billion in revenues over its term" in exchange for an "unenforceable promise" that a gas pipeline might be built.

"That approach is no more acceptable now than it was before AGIA," the governor told Mulva.

In her Jan. 15, 2008, state-of-the-state address to the Legislature the governor said: "Without AGIA's requirements, we'd be leveraged by a small group of companies. We can't surrender revenue, judicial process and our sovereignty.

"AGIA works," she said, telling legislators that TransCanada, a respected pipeline construction company, submitted a proposal under AGIA that met all of the state's requirements.

One good project

"We've long stated that it would only take one good application," the governor said Jan. 4, 2008, in announcing that TransCanada Alaska and Foothills Pipelines had submitted the only application found complete under AGIA. "And without presupposing the next phase of the process, we believe today that we have that application."

Legislators appeared to be less certain.

House Speaker John Harris, R-Valdez, quoted a letter from Tom Irwin, Marty Rutherford and Mark Myers, telling a Jan. 15 press conference that in December 2005 the three wrote: "Just getting the gas pipeline is not enough. It must be the best project for Alaska. If only one contract is moved forward to the Legislature, Alaskans may be deprived ... of the opportunity to choose the best project."

Reading from the 2005 letter Harris continued: "All options to get Alaska's gas to market should receive full consideration by the public and the Legislature, including proposals by the producers, TransCanada and the Alaska Gasline Port Authority."

Harris said he wanted to hear from the all-Alaska gas line proposal and any other projects, including ConocoPhillips.

"It's our understanding that it does not fit the framework of the law (AGIA) but it is still a proposal that ought to be considered and looked at by the Legislature to see if there are good points about it."

The Legislature has the right to change the law, he said, and if the ConocoPhillips proposal "gained traction" in the Legislature, the Legislature could change the law.

House Majority Leader Ralph Samuels, R-Anchorage, chair of

the Legislative Budget and Audit Committee, said the committee had attorneys and consultants looking at specific issues including the ConocoPhillips proposal and a potential liability from former TransCanada partners.

"As you all know I wasn't a big fan of the process. I still stand by my vote on AGIA. I still think we have some serious flaws," Samuels said. He also said that TransCanada is "a very real company ... they have a lot of pipe in the ground; they know how to build pipelines." He said he'd met with TransCanada officials over the years and "they've always been in my view pretty straight shooters."

BP, ConocoPhillips begin Denali work

April 8, while the administration was analyzing whether to recommend an AGIA license for TransCanada, BP and ConocoPhillips announced a joint venture gas pipeline from the North Slope to Alberta, and on to the Lower 48 if necessary.

Called Denali—The Alaska Gas Pipeline, the project was projected to cost $600 million to get to open season in late 2010 or early 2011, and as much as $30 billion for the project.

Jim Bowles, president of ConocoPhillips Alaska, and Doug Suttles, president of BP Exploration (Alaska), said field work for the line would begin in the summer of 2008, with an open season planned within 36 months.

Jim Bowles

"It sounds great for the State of Alaska; we're very excited about this announcement," Palin said at a press conference later that day. "I think this further proves that competition does work, that

Doug Suttles

AGIA being built on competition and ultimately allowing choices for Alaskans, the resource owners, now we can finally commercialize this gas up on the North Slope that we've been talking about and dreaming about for 50 years."

She said there had been rumors that something like this was in the works, and had been briefed earlier in the day by Bowles and Suttles.

The state's constitution mandates resource development consistent with the public interest for the maximum benefit of the people of Alaska, she said: "Whichever project gets us there first—in Alaska's best interest—is what we'll be supporting."

And while the governor said it sounded good that Denali was going forward without any state inducement, the state needed to determine what the companies would ask of the state. If it's "billions and billions of dollars" that would not be in the state's benefit. "We have to see if ... those tradeoffs are there," she said.

Fiscal discussion later

The companies said fiscal certainty from the State of Alaska would need to be addressed before an open season when the pipeline would ask shippers to make long-term gas commitments to the line.

Bowles said when the governor declined Conoco's 2007 proposal she asked that "before any discussion on a fiscal framework takes place that both ourselves and the state better understand what the costs of this project might be." He said that is what the companies were doing, with the expectation that a fiscal discussion with the state would take place before open season.

Suttles said BP had been "encouraged by the number of people who have spoken out and recognized that there are fiscal issues to sort out." That, he said, gave BP "the confidence that we can now actually move it forward and that people will work with us to solve the issues to get this gas moving."

Bowles said fiscal certainty was something pipeline owners expect to be necessary to "give future shippers confidence to make that 20- or 25-year shipping commitment."

The pipeline needed to "put together a project which will attract customers," Suttles said, "because without customers there won't be a line and there won't be the ability to build a line." That will require the most efficient project.

"I think our customers are going to be looking for a number of things to make sure that they're going to get an adequate return and I expect the fiscal issues to be part of that," Suttles said.

He said BP is "pretty confident" that over the next three years people will work the fiscal issue.

"If we didn't actually believe that, we wouldn't be doing this."

The shipping commitment will probably be in excess of $100 billion, Bowles said, and "any group of companies before making that type of commitment would want to understand that they've got a very predictable fiscal framework in front of them."

TransCanada recommendation

On May 22 Palin announced that TransCanada's AGIA application maximized benefits to Alaskans and recommended that the Alaska Legislature approve issuance of a license.

What had been a six-month closed-door analysis under AGIA moved into the public arena, with a three-day forum in Anchorage May 28-30, followed by special sessions of the Legislature which began June 3 and included hearings in Juneau and throughout the state.

"After decades of Alaskans dreaming about a pipeline that would transport Alaska's natural gas into really hungry markets, this administration has a plan in hand that will move Alaska's gas pipeline project forward, and quickly, and it is time," Palin, flanked by commissioners Irwin and Galvin and DNR Deputy Commissioner Marty Rutherford, who headed up the gas team, told a packed press conference May 22.

The news was good for TransCanada, but not for proponents of an LNG project, although the governor credited them with

Opening the Alaska Gasline Determination Public Forum, (left) Natural Resources Deputy Commissioner Marty Rutherford, (background) Natural Resources Commissioner Tom Irwin, (to the right of Rutherford, but only partly visible) Alaska Gov. Sarah Palin and (right) Revenue Commissioner Pat Galvin address questions from a crowded ballroom at the Anchorage Sheraton on May 28, 2008. The three days of presentations detailed the TC Alaska gas line proposal to legislators and the public in advance of the June 2008 legislative special session.

spurring a gas pipeline forward and "reminding Alaskans who owns these resources and what our constitution says about ownership. They get credit for bringing the gas line this far."

Palin said while there is enough natural gas for both an overland pipe into Canada (the TransCanada project) and LNG, analysis of LNG projects the gas line team did showed "LNG still has many, many challenges when compared to an overland route," which is both quicker and more economic.

Galvin said what came out in the analysis of the highway route vs. LNG "was extremely revealing and new." LNG projects do not provide the same reward to the state as the TransCanada project, Galvin said. Provided with expert information on LNG projects, the state found that they are complex and difficult to put together, with a "number of hurdles that are inherently in place for any LNG project to succeed."

Even if an LNG project had matched the economics of
TransCanada, "the likelihood of success of the LNG project would
have left it behind the TransCanada proposal," Galvin said. In both
economics and the likelihood of success, the TransCanada project
was superior to LNG, he said.

LNG not dead

The governor said LNG "is not dead, not by any stretch of the
imagination." She said an LNG project would work in conjunction
with TransCanada, and approving the TransCanada proposal "is
actually the best way to keep LNG alive," because if demand is high
enough, TransCanada would ship gas for an LNG project, down a
Y-line to Prince William Sound.

Irwin, fired by the previous administration because he disagreed
with their negotiations, said the gas team spent endless hours on the
analysis and did it right.

"We didn't approach it with any preconceived ideas," he said.
"We have done our homework," and that information will be
shared with Alaskans and with the Legislature. "The reasons
(behind the decision) are defensible," Irwin said.

He said the administration wanted both the state and the North
Slope producers to do well, but these are business issues.
"Sometimes we agree on these business issues and sometimes we're
in conflict; it doesn't mean we're enemies—these are business
issues," Irwin said.

Rutherford addressed the incentives issue—one that came to the
fore after the Denali project was announced in April.

AGIA upstream incentives were valuable to producers, she said.
If the state was going to provide value—"move values from our side
of the ledger to their side of the ledger, what we need in return is
protection on open access."

There are already values for those committing gas in AGIA "and
if at the end of the day people believe that something additional is
necessary then certainly the administration and the Legislature will

have that discussion. But we need to protect our interests in doing so."

Tony Palmer, TransCanada vice president of Alaska development, said when TransCanada built its first gas pipeline in Western Canada there were 180 wells, and today between 13,000 and 16,000 gas wells are completed each year.

"We clearly expect that with a project in service there will be significant new gas developed in this basin, as there has been in every other basin across North America once people know there's going to be a pipe in the ground," he said. Proven reserves in western Canada quadrupled within 10 years of TransCanada's initial pipeline going in, he said, and while TransCanada doesn't know the geology of the North Slope, "we do think it's a very prolific basin and can also see significant development once in service."

Kvisle comes to call

Hal Kvisle, president and CEO of TransCanada Corp., was in Anchorage May 29, meeting with Palin and legislators at the governor's AGIA public forum.

TransCanada has "been in pursuit of a solution for the Alaska gas pipeline project for many, many years," and was involved in the original project in the 1980s. The company resumed work on the Alaska project in 2000, 2001, he said at a press briefing.

Hal Kvisle

"It was quite clear from our work that supply-demand fundamentals for natural gas in North America were moving in a direction where there would be a scarcity of natural gas," and the company focused on Alaska and the Mackenzie Valley as "projects that could bring significant gas to a market that we felt was going to increasingly need it."

In addition to its proposal to the State of Alaska under AGIA, "we've worked closely with the Alaskan producers over the past seven or eight years to try to come up with a solution that would

May: Palin focused on gas line

Alaska Gov. Sarah Palin said May 29, 2008, she thought rumors she was being considered as a vice presidential running mate for John McCain were circulating because of the interest in Alaska's gas pipeline.

Attention was on her administration "because of what is going on here in Alaska; when you're looking at this gas line, when you're looking at what Alaska is ready to produce and contribute to the rest of the U.S., there are a lot of eyes on Alaska right now," she said.

The governor said she'd recently done interviews with Forbes, the New York Times, the Wall Street Journal and Newsweek.

They were "not ... necessarily looking at me," she said, "but looking at what the heck is going on up there in Alaska."

The interest is because there's "a lot of moving and shaking in Alaska and it is all about our resources" and the state's willingness to get those resources to markets.

As for her interest in the vice presidential slot, Palin said: "I'm interested in getting a gas line. ... Working with our good lawmakers here, it's going to happen; and I think that that is the way that Alaska will be able to contribute to the U.S. ... that's what we're focused on and I think I can help do that."

enable this gas to get to market," Kvisle said. He called the structure developed under AGIA "a very solid approach to moving this project forward."

The next step is legislative approval of the AGIA license, he said, and then TransCanada will move on to finalize commercial elements.

Getting the North Slope gas producers to sign on with TransCanada will require developing "a commercial arrangement that they will find attractive, a commercial arrangement for the shipment of gas through the pipeline that will appeal to the North Slope producers, and ... we're committed to doing that," Kvisle said.

It's "a collaborative process," he said. "We have to be able to offer something that they find appealing, but that I think is something I think we're pretty good at. We didn't become the largest mover of natural gas in North America without having good relations with our customers," Kvisle said. "That's important."

He said all big pipeline projects involve government, "a pipeline company that knows how to get the job done and producers that own the gas—and a marketplace that wants the gas. And as I look at the Alaska project I see all of those elements falling into place, but I don't understate for a minute it's a lot of work to get there."

Gas commitment remains an issue

The BP-ConocoPhillips Denali pipeline proposal attracted legislators because it solved the issue of getting gas in the pipeline.

Palin said May 22 that there was no reason to think the producers wouldn't want to commit gas to an economic AGIA project. "They're reasonable commercial players," she said, and are looking out for the bottom line.

Galvin said May 23 at an Alaska State Chamber of Commerce-Resource Development Council discussion that if the state were to set aside AGIA and go with the Denali project, that "puts the state at tremendous risk, tremendous risk that the project's not going to advance until the state provides some sort of additional fiscal concessions; the risk that the fiscal concession is going to be tremendously expensive to the state; or the risk that no fiscal concession is ultimately going to result in those commitments."

And if the producers went ahead and built Denali and committed their gas without state concessions, the state would still be better off "than if we had provided them with potentially billions of dollars of concessions," Galvin said, referring to an estimate of a $10 billion price tag put on the cost to the state of the fiscal contract negotiated by the Murkowski administration.

He said the AGIA protections ensure gas exploration because without them new companies won't have assurance of getting their gas into a line.

"And the risk isn't that we're going to end up knowing that the pipeline that didn't have these AGIA protections resulted in killing off a bunch of new wells that would otherwise have been drilled because frankly we'll never know.

"It's all the people that never showed up."

Extensive legislative hearings

The Legislature discussed the TransCanada AGIA license, along with the governor's proposal to address high energy costs by sending an additional $1,200 to each Alaskan qualified for the 2008 Permanent Fund Dividend, over two special sessions.

Galvin said in September 2008 that he couldn't find anyone who could tell him of a similar situation, where House and Senate sat jointly (in sessions chaired by the House Rules Committee and the Senate's Special Committee on Energy) for some 45 days in June and July questioning the administration, TransCanada, representatives of the producers and Denali, and consultants for both the administration and the Legislature.

What may have been a telling discussion happened early on, when on June 5 Dan Dickinson, a former head of the Department of Revenue's tax division employed by legislators to help them examine the issues, told legislators he didn't think any harm could come from approving the AGIA license.

Dickinson said there have been five major reasons given for supporting the TransCanada AGIA license: It provides enforceable commitments the state hasn't had before; it makes what has been described as a "dazzling" amount of money for everyone, so it seems logical that producers would sign on and the project would advance; it "guarantees" the state's must haves for an "enhanced open-access pipeline" as opposed to the open access pipeline created by federal law; it is not in competition with an LNG project, and in fact may be the best way of getting an LNG export project once the mainline is operating; and voting for the license is the best way of meeting in-state gas needs.

Moreover, he said: Granting an AGIA license to TransCanada "probably won't harm the prospects for a line and may strengthen them." We're on our own one- or two-yard line, Dickinson told legislators, and while it's important to do it right, this won't be a

TransCanada Vice President Tony Palmer, Alaska Gov. Sarah Palin, Natural Resources Commissioner Tom Irwin, Natural Resources Deputy Commissioner Marty Rutherford and Revenue Commissioner Pat Galvin address the media at an Aug. 1, 2008, press conference after the legislature awarded TC Alaska the AGIA license to move forward and build Alaska's natural gas pipeline.

touchdown play. He said he didn't see any huge downside in voting for the license.

The other Legislative Budget and Audit Committee consultants testifying agreed that they could see no harm in the license.

License passes

In the end, in spite of opposition from Republican leadership in both House and Senate, the Alaska Legislature approved giving an AGIA license to TransCanada.

The House voted 24-16 to approve the license July 22, but on a reconsideration vote July 23 the immediate effective date in the bill did not pass, defaulting the effective date to a constitutional 90 days after the governor's signature. The license could not be issued until the bill was effective; any work done by TransCanada before the license is issued would not be eligible for matching funds from the state.

The House also voted unanimously to approve a letter of intent to accompany the bill, urging the executive branch to continue "to aid project proposals in addition to just a TransCanada pipeline into Canada."

"It is the intent of the Legislature that an AGIA license will enable and encourage an All Alaska gas line/liquefied natural gas (LNG) project within the TransCanada project," the letter said.

TransCanada said in its AGIA application that if there was gas committed to go to Valdez for an LNG project, it would build that line, although it did not commit to build a liquefied natural gas facility at Valdez, just to transport gas if there was a shipper wanting to go to Valdez.

While AGIA only edged out of the Senate Special Committee on Energy by a 7-5 vote, it passed handily on the Senate floor by a vote of 14-5 on Aug. 1.

It took legislative leadership a while to forward the bill to Palin, but she was finally able to sign it into law Aug. 27.

Palin said the legislation brought the state "miles closer than we have ever been to building that natural gas pipeline, finally accessing our gas that's been warehoused for so many decades up on the North Slope.

"This legislation will create jobs and provide income for Alaskans for years to come," the governor said.

"Being involved in government is what I was created to do."

—gubernatorial candidate Sarah Palin,
Mat-Su Valley Frontiersman, March 2006